10th Workshop on Natural Language Processing for Computer Assisted Language Learning (NLP4CALL 2021)

Online
31 May 2021

Editors:

David Alfter
Elena Volodina
Ildikó Pilán
Johannes Graën
Lars Borin

ISBN: 978-1-7138-9189-5

Printed from e-media with permission by:

Curran Associates, Inc.
57 Morehouse Lane
Red Hook, NY 12571

Some format issues inherent in the e-media version may also appear in this print version.

Printed with permission by Curran Associates, Inc. (2024)

For permission requests, please contact the Association for Computational Linguistics at the address below.

Association for Computational Linguistics
209 N. Eighth Street
Stroudsburg, Pennsylvania 18360

Phone: 1-570-476-8006
Fax: 1-570-476-0860

acl@aclweb.org

Additional copies of this publication are available from:

Curran Associates, Inc.
57 Morehouse Lane
Red Hook, NY 12571 USA
Phone: 845-758-0400
Fax: 845-758-2633
Email: curran@proceedings.com
Web: www.proceedings.com

NEALT Proceedings Series Vol. 47

Proceedings of the 10th Workshop on Natural Language Processing for Computer Assisted Language Learning (NLP4CALL 2021)

Linköping Electronic Conference Proceedings 177
eISSN 1650-3740 (Online) • ISSN 1650-3686 (Print) 2021

Proceedings of the

10th Workshop on Natural Language Processing for Computer Assisted Language Learning (NLP4CALL 2021)

edited by

David Alfter, Elena Volodina, Ildikó Pilán, Johannes Graën
and Lars Borin

Linköping Electronic Conference Proceedings 177
eISSN 1650-3740 (Online) • ISSN 1650-3686 (Print) 2021

Preface

The workshop series on Natural Language Processing (NLP) for Computer-Assisted Language Learning (NLP4CALL) is a meeting place for researchers working on the integration of Natural Language Processing and Speech Technologies in CALL systems and exploring the theoretical and methodological issues arising in this connection. The latter includes, among others, the integration of insights from Second Language Acquisition (SLA) research, and the promotion of "Computational SLA" through setting up Second Language research infrastructures.

The intersection of Natural Language Processing (or Language Technology / Computational Linguistics) and Speech Technology with Computer-Assisted Language Learning (CALL) brings "understanding" of language to CALL tools, thus making CALL intelligent. This fact has given the name for this area of research – Intelligent CALL, or for short, ICALL. As the definition suggests, apart from having excellent knowledge of Natural Language Processing and/or Speech Technology, ICALL researchers need good insights into second language acquisition theories and practices, as well as knowledge of second language pedagogy and didactics. This workshop therefore invites a wide range of ICALL-relevant research, including studies where NLP-enriched tools are used for testing SLA and pedagogical theories, and vice versa, where SLA theories, pedagogical practices or empirical data and modelled in ICALL tools. The NLP4CALL workshop series is aimed at bringing together competences from these areas for sharing experiences and brainstorming around the future of the field.

We invited submissions:

- that describe research directly aimed at ICALL
- that demonstrate actual or discuss the potential use of existing Language and Speech Technologies or resources for language learning
- that describe the ongoing development of resources and tools with potential usage in ICALL, either directly in interactive applications, or indirectly in materials, application, or curriculum development, e.g. learning material generation, assessment of learner texts and responses, individualized learning solutions, provision of feedback
- that discuss challenges and/or research agenda for ICALL
- that describe empirical studies on language learner data

This year a special focus was given to work done on second language vocabulary and grammar profiling, as well as the use of crowdsourcing for creating, collecting, and curating data in NLP projects. We encouraged paper presentations and software demonstrations describing the above-mentioned themes primarily, but not exclusively, for the Nordic languages.

A special feature in this year's workshop is the *research notes* session. This session included short talks about PhD projects and ongoing unfinished research that collaborating teams were eager to discuss with the community and get feedback. We tested this feature for the second time with an intention to evaluate its impact and utility for future uses. This time around, we circulated a separate call for expression of interest.

This year, we had the pleasure to welcome two invited speakers: Mark Brenchley (Cambridge Assessment English; co-presenter: Kevin Cheung, Cambridge Assessment English) and Johanna Monti (University of Naples).

Dr **Mark Brenchley** is Senior Research Manager at Cambridge Assessment English. Mark manages research supporting the development and validation of Cambridge English products in the areas of speaking and writing, as well as vocabulary and grammar more broadly. He specialises in the application of corpus-based methodologies and is responsible for maintaining and developing the company's internal corpus architecture, including the Cambridge Learner Corpus. His current work, in particular, focuses on the development and validation of auto-marking technologies.

David Alfter, Elena Volodina, Ildikó Pilán, Johannes Graën and Lars Borin 2021. Preface. *Proceedings of the 10th Workshop on Natural Language Processing for Computer Assisted Language Learning (NLP4CALL 2021)*. Linköping Electronic Conference Proceedings 177: i–iv.

In his talk, *What is an NLP NLP? Considerations from an L2 Assessment Perspective*, he offered a more philosophical perspective on the role of NLP in second language assessment, focusing on the question of what it might actually mean for something to be an "NLP NLP"; that is, a natural language processed, natural language profile. In general, he explored the relationship between NLP and L2 profiles with regard to the wider notion of validity as a key assessment concept.

Dr **Johanna Monti** is currently Associate Professor and Third Mission Delegate at the L'Orientale University of Naples, where she teaches Translation Studies, Specialised Translation, Computational Linguistics for Translation, Machine and Computer Aided Translation. She received her PhD in Theories, Methodologies and Advanced applications for Communication, Computer Science and Physics with a thesis in Computational Linguistics at the University of Salerno, Italy. She the Chief Scientist of the UNIOR NLP Research Group, node in Natural Language Processing and Computational Linguistics of the CINI Italian Lab on Artificial Intelligence and Intelligent Systems. Her current research activities are in the field of Machine Translation, the impact of MT in the translation process, the evaluation of the new translation technologies and finally new methodologies in the development of linguistic data for NLP & CALL applications.

In her talk, *Challenges of Gamified Crowdsourcing for language learning applications*, she presented an overview of different types of gamified crowdsourcing and discuss the emerging opportunities and challenges of using it for language learning applications.

Previous workshops

This workshop follows a series of workshops on NLP4CALL organized by the NEALT Special Interest Group on Intelligent Computer-Assisted Language Learning (SIG-ICALL[1]). The workshop series has previously been financed by the Center for Language Technology at the University of Gothenburg, the SweLL project[2], and the Swedish Research Council's conference grant. Currently the funding comes from Språkbanken Text[3] and the L2 profiling project[4].

Submissions to the ten workshop editions have targeted a wide range of languages, ranging from well-resourced languages (Chinese, German, English, French, Portuguese, Russian, Spanish) to lesser-resourced languages (Erzya, Arabic, Estonian, Irish, Komi-Zyrian, Meadow Mari, Saami, Udmurt, Võro). Among these, several Nordic languages have been targeted, namely Danish, Estonian, Finnish, Icelandic, Norwegian, Saami, Swedish and Võro. The wide scope of the workshop is also evident in the affiliations of the participating authors as illustrated in Table 1.

Country	2012-2020 (# speaker/co-author affiliations)
Algeria	1
Australia	2
Belgium	5
Canada	4
Cyprus	2
Denmark	3
Egypt	1
Estonia	3
Finland	10

[1] https://spraakbanken.gu.se/en/research/themes/icall/sig-icall
[2] https://spraakbanken.gu.se/en/projects/swell
[3] https://spraakbanken.gu.se
[4] https://spraakbanken.gu.se/en/projects/l2profiles

France	9
Germany	89
Iceland	6
Ireland	2
Italy	7
Japan	5
Lithuania	1
Netherlands	4
Norway	13
Portugal	6
Romania	1
Russia	10
Slovakia	1
Spain	3
Sweden	67
Switzerland	10
UK	11
US	7

Table 1. NLP4CALL speakers' and co-authors' affiliations, 2012-2021

The acceptance rate has varied between 50% and 77%, the average being 63% (see Table 2).

Although the acceptance rate is rather high, the reviewing process has always been very rigorous with two to three double-blind reviews per submission. This indicates that submissions to the workshop have usually been of high quality.

Workshop year	Submitted	Accepted	Acceptance rate
2012	12	8	67%
2013	8	4	50%
2014	13	10	77%
2015	9	6	67%
2016	14	10	72%
2017	13	7	54%
2018	16	11	69%
2019	16	10	63%
2020	7	4	57%
2021	11	6	54%

Table 2: Submissions and acceptance rates, 2012-2021

We would like to thank our Program Committee for providing detailed feedback for the reviewed papers:

- David Alfter, University of Gothenburg, Sweden
- Claudia Borg, University of Malta, Malta
- António Branco, Universidade de Lisboa, Portugal
- Andrew Caines, University of Cambridge, UK
- Xiaobin Chen, Universität Tübingen, Germany
- Kordula de Kuthy, Universität Tübingen, Germany
- Simon Dobnik, University of Gothenburg, Sweden
- Thomas François, Université catholique de Louvain, Belgium
- Johannes Graën, University of Gothenburg, Sweden and University of Zurich, Switzerland
- Andrea Horbach, University of Duisburg-Essen, Germany
- Ronja Laarman-Quante, University of Duisburg-Essen, Germany

- Herbert Lange, University of Gothenburg, Sweden and Chalmers Institute of Technology, Sweden
- Peter Ljunglöf, University of Gothenburg, Sweden and Chalmers Institute of Technology, Sweden
- Verena Lyding, EURAC research, Italy
- Detmar Meurers, Universität Tübingen, Germany
- Margot Mieskes, University of Applied Sciences Darmstadt, Germany
- Lionel Nicolas, EURAC research, Italy
- Robert Östling, Stockholm University, Sweden
- Ulrike Pado, Hochschule für Technik Stuttgart, Germany
- Magali Paquot, Université catholique de Louvain, Belgium
- Ildikó Pilán, Norwegian Computing Center, Norway
- Gerold Schneider, University of Zurich, Switzerland
- Egon Stemle, EURAC research, Italy
- Anaïs Tack, Université catholique de Louvain, Belgium and KU Leuven, Belgium
- Irina Temnikova, Mitra Translations, Bulgaria
- Sowmya Vajjala, National Research Council, Canada
- Elena Volodina, University of Gothenburg, Sweden
- Zarah Weiss, Universität Tübingen, Germany
- Victoria Yaneva, National Board of Medical Examiners, Philadelphia, USA
- Torsten Zesch, University of Duisburg-Essen, Germany
- Ramon Ziai, Universität Tübingen, Germany

We intend to continue this workshop series, which so far has been the only ICALL-relevant recurring event based in the Nordic countries. Our intention is to co-locate the workshop series with the two major LT events in Scandinavia, SLTC (the Swedish Language Technology Conference) and NoDaLiDa (Nordic Conference on Computational Linguistics), thus making this workshop an annual event. Through this workshop, we intend to profile ICALL research in Nordic countries as well as beyond, and we aim at providing a dissemination venue for researchers active in this area.

Workshop website:

https://spraakbanken.gu.se/forskning/teman/icall/nlp4call-workshop-series/nlp4call2021

Workshop organizers

David Alfter[1], Elena Volodina[1], Ildikó Pilán[2], Johannes Graën[1,3], Lars Borin[1]

[1] Språkbanken, University of Gothenburg, Sweden

[2] Norwegian Computing Center, Norway

[3] Department of Computational Linguistics, University of Zurich, Switzerland

Acknowledgements

We gratefully acknowledge the financial support from *Språkbanken Text* and the *L2 profiles for Swedish* project.

Contents

An Experiment on Implicitly Crowdsourcing Expert Knowledge about Romanian Synonyms from L1 Language Learners

Lionel Nicolas[1], **Lavinia Aparaschivei**[1], **Verena Lyding**[1], **Christos Rodosthenous**[2], **Federico Sangati**[3], **Alexander König**[5], **Corina Forascu**[4]

[1]Institute for Applied Linguistics, Eurac Research, Bolzano, Italy
[2]Computational Cognition Lab, Open University of Cyprus, Cyprus
[3]Cognitive Neurorobotics Research Unit, Okinawa Institute of Science and Technology, Japan
[4] Faculty of Computer Science, Alexandru Ioan Cuza University of Iasi, Romania
[5]CLARIN ERIC, the Netherlands

Abstract

In this paper, we present an experiment performed with the aim of evaluating if linguistic knowledge of expert quality about Romanian synonyms could be crowdsourced from L1 language learners, learning Romanian as their mother tongue, by collecting and aggregating their answers to two types of questions that are automatically generated from a dataset, encoding semantic relations between words. Such an evaluation aimed at confirming the viability of a fully learner-fueled crowdsourcing workflow for improving such type of dataset. For this experiment, we reused an existing open-source crowdsourcing vocabulary trainer that we designed for this very purpose and which crowdsourcing potential needed further evaluation, especially with regards to lesser-resourced languages such as Romanian. Our results confirmed that producing expert knowledge regarding Romanian synonyms could be achieved in such a fashion. Additionally, we took the occasion to further evaluate the learning impact of the trainer on the participants and gather their feedback regarding several aspects.

1 Introduction

The lack of Linguistic Resources (LRs) and the lack of exercise content are respectively two long-standing issues that are slowing down the domains of Natural Language Processing (NLP) and Computer-Assisted Language Learning (CALL). Recent efforts that implement an implicit crowdsourcing paradigm have started to tackle these issues in a concurrent fashion (Nicolas et al., 2020). Such a paradigm follows the idea that if a dataset can be used to generate the content of a specific type of exercise, then the answers to these exercises can also be used to improve back the dataset that allowed to generate the exercise content.

Among the efforts implementing this paradigm, we devised an open-source and publicly-available vocabulary trainer called v-trel (Rodosthenous et al., 2019; Lyding et al., 2019; Rodosthenous et al., 2020) in order to generate exercises from a knowledge-base called ConceptNet (Speer et al., 2017) while using the crowdsourced answers to improve ConceptNet. In the experiments we previously conducted and reported about, we provided some preliminary evidence towards its crowdsourcing potential but a more thorough investigation was still needed, especially with regards to a lesser-resourced language such as Romanian that is far less represented in ConceptNet. Furthermore, the evaluation of the learning impact of v-trel on its users also had room for further exploration. For this experiment, we aimed at filling both gaps, while taking the opportunity to gather more feedback about the vocabulary trainer.

We explain hereafter how we demonstrated that aggregating the partial and neophyte knowledge of L1 learners of Romanian[1] could be used to pro-

[1]The experiment originally targeted L2 students but the health crisis due to the Covid-19 pandemic limited our networking options and we had to rely on already established

Lionel Nicolas, Lavinia Nicoleta Aparaschivei, Verena Lyding, Christos Rodosthenous, Federico Sangati, Alexander König and Corina Forascu 2021. An experiment on implicitly crowdsourcing expert knowledge about Romanian synonyms from language learners. *Proceedings of the 10th Workshop on Natural Language Processing for Computer Assisted Language Learning (NLP4CALL 2021)*. Linköping Electronic Conference Proceedings 177: 1–14.

duce knowledge of expert quality about Romanian synonyms. We therefore explain how our experiment provides evidence that v-trel, and its underlying approach in general, can be used to devise a fully learner-powered crowdsourcing workflow for improving datasets, encoding semantic relations between words. We also explain how this experiment allowed us to gather additional insights regarding the learning impact on the participants.

This paper is organized as follows. In Section 2, we present work related to our approach and discuss similarities. Next, in Section 3, we briefly discuss v-trel and the gaps we aimed at filling with this experiment. In Section 4, we explain how we adapted v-trel for the purpose of our experiment, and in Section 5 we describe how we set up our experiment. We then discuss the results we achieved in Section 6. Finally, we explore future efforts in Section 7 and conclude in Section 8.

2 Related work

Our efforts are situated at the crossroad between crowdsourcing knowledge in order to enhance linguistic resources and automatically generating exercises for CALL purposes. Accordingly, the relevant state of the art is composed of approaches targeting only one or both of the two subjects.

With respect to the previous work related only to the automatic generation of exercises, the state of the art is composed of only a handful of approaches that generate exercises directly from linguistic resources. Most related works actually focus on the "cloze" (deletion) test, where a portion of the text has some of the words automatically removed by some NLP-based pipeline, and the learner is asked to recover the missing words (Lee et al., 2019; Hill and Simha, 2016). In Lyding et al. (2019), we confirmed the lack of automatic generation of exercises based on linguistic resources by reviewing the most recent proceedings of two CALL-oriented NLP workshops[2] and coming to the conclusion that current efforts are dedicated to other subjects such as the generation of cloze exercises, the modelling of the learner knowledge, or the detection and/or correction of mistakes in written productions. Among recent work targeting the generation of language learning exercises, we can point to Chinkina et al. (2017) and Chinkina et al. (2020), in which the authors addressed the development of a novel form of automatic generation of questions that combines a wh-question with gapped sentences. Following a small-scale pilot study, the work of Ziegler et al. (2017) provided empirical evidence supporting the effectiveness of instructional treatments, such as input enhancement, for L2 growth, as well as exploring how technological innovations could deepen our understanding of L2 acquisition. We can also refer to the work presented by De Kuthy et al. (2020), in which the authors described an automatic question generation approach to partially automate *Questions under Discussion* (QUD) annotation by generating all potentially relevant questions for a given sentence in a German text. In addition, in Fenogenova and Kuzmenko (2016), the authors proposed an approach to automated generation of English lexical exercises for learning collocations, and then compared the exercises produced to those compiled manually by language instructors.

Regarding the previous works related only to the crowdsourcing of linguistic resources, they can mostly be categorized into two groups aiming at curating a varied set of linguistic resources: the approaches relying on micro-task platforms (e.g. Kordoni et al. (2016), Caines et al. (2016), Lafourcade (2007), Ganbold et al. (2018), Post et al. (2012)), and the approaches implementing implicit crowdsourcing approaches that crowdsource information from a crowd that is not necessarily aware of the on-going crowdsourcing. This is usually achieved by embedding the implicit crowdsourcing approach into a workflow used for a different purpose than crowdsourcing. For example, among approaches implementing implicit crowdsourcing methods, a great share of the state of the art consists in games that implicitly crowdsource linguistic knowledge from their users while providing them entertainment. Such games are referred to as GWAPs (Games with a Purpose) and include efforts such as Lafourcade (2007), Poesio et al. (2013) or Guillaume et al. (2016)).

Finally, with regards to previous works related to both the automatic generation of language learning exercises and the crowdsourcing of linguistic resources, the state of the art contains only a limited number of efforts that combine both as we do. The most famous initiative is certainly

contacts with schools instructing L1 Romanian students that, despite being proficient, are still learning their mother tongue (see proficiency results in Section 6).

[2] Innovative Use of NLP for Building Educational Applications (Tetreault et al., 2018) and NLP for Computer Assisted Language Learning (Alfter et al., 2019).

Duolingo (von Ahn, 2013) which used to generate translation exercises and crowdsourced the answers to sell them later to third parties. Other efforts were developed in the context of the enetCollect COST Action and implement the aforementioned implicit crowdsourcing paradigm (Nicolas et al., 2020). V-trel is one of them and, as a cornerstone of our work, we discuss it in greater details in the following section. Among the other works related to enetCollect and/or the implicit crowdsourcing paradigm, we can also point the readers to Millour et al. (2019), Smrz (2019), Grace Araneta et al. (2020) and Arhar Holdt et al. (2021) that all aimed at crowdsourcing lexical knowledge. Finally, two other learning tools are also worth considering: one for crowdsourcing POS corpora (Sangati et al., 2015) and another one for crowdsourcing syntactic dependencies (Hladká et al., 2014).

3 v-trel in a nutshell

The vocabulary trainer v-trel is a prototypical language learning tool that generates vocabulary exercises from a multilingual linguistic resource called ConceptNet (Speer et al., 2017) in which words and their semantic relations to one another are recorded (e.g. translation, synonyms, hypernyms etc.) in the form of triples ($word_1$, relation, $word_2$). At the same time, v-trel crowdsources the answers with the aim of producing through aggregation an expert knowledge that can be used to enhance ConceptNet. V-trel offers exercises through a user-friendly chatbot interface accessible from the Telegram messenger[3].

V-trel generates two types of exercises: *open exercises* in which users are provided a word and asked to provide another one related to the first one by a specific semantic relation (e.g. *provide a synonym of "house"*) and *closed exercises* in which users are asked if a pair of words are related to one another according to a specific type of semantic relation (e.g., *Are "home" and "house" synonyms?*).

The version of v-trel we adapted for our experiment generates open exercises from a finite list of words and the closed exercises from both the recurrent triples suggested by learners in answers to open exercises and the existing triples already encoded in ConceptNet. By proceeding in such a fashion, the answers provided to the closed questions can be aggregated and used to, on the one hand, validate or discard triples suggested in open exercises to extend ConceptNet and, on the other hand, validate or contradict the triples already encoded. The user feedback to open questions is based both on the answer previously provided by other learners and on the existence of a matching triple in ConceptNet. User feedback to closed questions exclusively relies on the presence (or absence) of a matching triple in ConceptNet. In order to support the learners in their efforts, v-trel also implements a number of user-oriented features such as a hint feature allowing to request examples, an automatically generated link to Wikipedia[4] allowing to swiftly consult a dedicated page on Wikipedia (if any) and a point system with a functionality displaying a leaderboard that allows learners to compete among themselves.

While the experiments we described in the two last papers about v-trel (Lyding et al., 2019; Rodosthenous et al., 2020) allowed us to validate and/or enhance many relevant aspects, no extensive formal proof was made that expert knowledge could indeed be derived from the answers of the learners. This is mainly due to the fact that for the last experiment reported, while we could confirm the capacity of open questions to generate relevant triples to include in ConceptNet, we generated a large number of closed questions that diluted the set of answers crowdsourced. This setup led to an insufficient average number of answers per closed question that prevented us from performing any kind of aggregation that could produce the expert knowledge needed to validate or discard new triples or existing ones. As a fallback approach for closed questions, we manually evaluated the quality of a random sample of answers in order to demonstrate that they were on average correct for more than 50% of them and that, consequently, expert quality would statistically have been achieved by collecting more answers. Nonetheless, we discovered after the experiment a bias toward positive answers in the responses of learners that prevented us from doing so. Indeed, since the closed exercises are both mostly automatically generated from the new triples recurrently suggested in open questions and the ones available in ConceptNet, the correct answer was in most case "Yes"[5] and learners grad-

[3]https://telegram.org/

[4]E.g. https://en.wikipedia.org/wiki/House for *house*

[5]There were also a few closed questions automatically

ually understood it over time[6]. Consequently, in order to earn more points, most learners chose to always answer positively in case of doubt instead of choosing the option "I-don't-know" that allowed them to skip a question for which they were not sure of the correct answer. As a consequence, whereas the average accuracy of the answers to closed exercises where the correct answer was "yes" was far above 50%, the average accuracy of the answers for the ones where the correct answer was "no" was under 50%. This issue thus prevented us to indirectly confirm the crowdsourcing potential. Another aspect for which the evaluation of the crowdsourcing potential is further explored with this new experiment is the language targeted. Indeed, only English, the language best covered in ConceptNet has been considered so far.

Regarding the learning impact on users, we evaluated the learning impact on users by relying on pre- and post-experiment vocabulary tests that were manually revised by an expert and also some small randomly sampled sets of answers of a few students. For the last experiment described in Rodosthenous et al. (2020), while results of the pre- and post-questionnaires were not conclusive, we observed some learning impact as the average accuracy of the small randomly sampled sets of answers of the most prolific five students were slightly better for the second half of the sets than for the first. However, the difference was not vast (+4%) and the size of the sample was limited (100 answers) and only concerned five learners. We thus explore this question in order to further support our previous findings.

4 Adapting v-trel

Overall, we adapted v-trel by partially disconnecting several automatic mechanisms in order to create a more static version that allowed us to better evaluate the aspects we were interested in. In that perspective, as our main focus was not so much to produce expert knowledge in order to improve ConceptNet but to produce it for the purpose of evaluating its quality, the crowdsourcing we made was more of a simulation of crowdsourcing since we asked many questions for which we knew the answers. Regarding the evaluation of the learning impact on learners, we did not adapt v-trel in any particular way as we relied on the evolution of the accuracy of the answers provided over time. We thus relied on an intrinsic evaluation instead of using an extrinsic approach such as one with pre- and post-tests.

The adaptations that we performed focused mainly on the open and closed questions and are discussed hereafter. Aside from these, we localized the interface to Romanian and used synonymy as the type of semantic relations on which the learners were tested.

Indeed, in our previous experiments on v-trel, we used the "relatedTo" relation between words in ConceptNet. A closed question could have for example be "is *home* related to *family*?". From the experience we gained so far, we concluded that finding consensual answers for some of these questions was more challenging than we originally thought. We thus chose to use synonymy instead which made the task far easier. The criteria we used to further specify our notion of synonyms was that two words shall be considered as synonyms of one another if they can be exchanged/paraphrased in a sentence without altering its overall meaning. For example the Romanian words "*imagine*" ("*picture*" in English) and "*ilustraţie*" ("*illustration*" in English) can freely be exchanged in the Romanian sentence "*Profesoara le-a aratat copiilor o ilustraţie/ imagine cu o expediţie de la Polul Nord.*" ("*The teacher showed the children an illustration/picture with an expedition from the North Pole.*" in English) without altering its overall meaning. The definition of synonymy we used is thus one that also accounts for partial synonymy between words that would probably not be considered as synonyms of one another if considered outside the context in a sentence.

4.1 Adapting the open questions

The open questions and the feedback given to the learners remained globally the same. Learners thus received points if they provided an answer that matched an existing triple in ConceptNet or if they provided answers that their fellow learners provided as well a sufficient number of times. Unlike our previous experiments, we post-evaluated the answers that were given more than twice by the learners, to observe if the frequency of occurrences of an answer was correlated with its quality (see Section 6).

generated from triple encoding a relation *NotRelatedTo* for which the correct answer was "No", but they were not numerous enough.

[6] Some learners actually said it explicitly in the user questionnaire they answered after the experiment.

We limited the number of open questions so as to avoid diluting the answers of learners. The size of the set of open questions was estimated by doing a mock-up test with a few people before the experiment that allowed us to estimate the average number of answers per person and per hour. We then multiplied this number by the number of participants expected and the average number of hours we expected them to contribute to our experiment.

4.2 Adapting the closed questions

Unlike the case of open questions, our adaptations focused on avoiding two issues: a too large number of closed questions that would dilute excessively the answers of learners, as well as an imbalance between closed questions for which the correct answer was "yes" and the ones for which the correct answer was "no" (in order to avoid influencing silently the learners in answering an option more than another as it happened in a previous experiment).

We addressed the first issue by generating a finite set of closed questions. The size of this set was also estimated via the mock-up test prior to the experiment. In order to maintain the size of this set of questions, we disconnected the mechanism that automatically generates closed questions from the answers provided to open questions.

In order to address the second issue and have a balanced set between closed questions for which the correct answer was "yes" and the ones for which the correct answer was "no", we automatically generated from ConceptNet two sets of closed questions, one for each type of answer, and a single annotator manually revised them in order to ensure that our final set was indeed balanced. We thus created for our experiment a specific gold standard for the closed questions and used it afterwards to study how much the aggregated knowledge extracted from the answers of the learners was correlated with it (see Section 6).

In order to automatically generate the two sets of closed questions to revise manually, we implemented and tested mechanisms exploring ConceptNet according to two assumptions that allowed us to create and rank two different lists: a list of potential pairs of synonyms and and a list of pairs of words that could be anything but synonyms of one another.

The assumption to generate potential pairs of synonyms is a well-known one that follows the idea that *If two Romanian words A and C are translations of the same word B in a different language, then A and C might be synonyms.* This assumption thus relies on semantic relations describing translations between words that, on a conceptual level, could be considered as relations describing pairs of synonyms belonging to different languages. For example, "frumos" and "atrăgător" are synonyms and both translate to "beautiful" in English. The ranking of the pairs of words included in the list generated is then based on the number of common translations (referred to as *B* before) found in all the languages.

The assumption to generate potential pairs of words that can be anything but synonyms of one another is that *If two Romanian words A and D are respectively both translations in a different language of two words B and C that have a relation that is not a synonymy relation (e.g. antonymy or hyperonymy), then A and D might have the same relation in Romanian and are most likely not synonyms of one another.* For example "flat" is a type of "home" in English and they translate to "apartament" and "casă" respectively in Romanian. The ranking of the pairs of words included in the list generated is then based on the size of the set of pairs of translations (referred to as *B* and *C* before) found in all languages. A valuable particularity of this mechanism is that the pairs of words were meaningful as they are part of the semantic landscape of one another, as opposed to a mechanism that would randomly pick two words (e.g. *bred* and *plane*).

A single annotator then revised in an orderly fashion the two lists until our gold standard had the size we aimed at. In order to make sure that open questions and closed questions have common grounds, we used the list of words of the open questions as word *A* in the two assumptions we relied on to generate closed questions.

Creating a gold standard for the closed questions also solved another issue: the feedback provided to the student for such questions. Indeed, v-trel relies at present on ConceptNet to provide such feedback. However, ConceptNet is a dataset that contains noise that can induce improper feedback to an extent that can create distrust from the users[7]. Should v-trel become fully functional, it

[7]By browsing the online version of ConceptNet, you'll see that, for example, *school* is marked as related to *sociotem-*

will over time be capable of gradually improving ConceptNet, or some specifically-selected parts of it, and thus reduce the noise it contains while enhancing its coverage. Since our experiment aimed at demonstrating the crowdsourcing potential of v-trel, relying on a gold standard for the closed questions allowed us to circumvent this issue.

5 Experimental setup

For our experiment, we generated 750 open questions and 1792 closed questions[8].

The experiment involved three classes with a total of 48 L1 students, aged between 18 and 19 years, that were taught Romanian by two teachers that agreed to support our initiative. The students were attending two high schools with different specializations, one theoretical and the other technical, respectively referred to as school "*1*" and "*2*" in Table 1. In order to foster participation and competition between the students, a contest to win vouchers for an e-commerce for the top five ranked participants, as listed on the leaderboard (see Section 3), was organized. Out of the 48 students, 20 registered and actively participated.

The experiment ran for 17 calendar days, from 28 May 2020 to 13 June 2020. The experiment was introduced by the teachers, who were always assisted by one of the authors, with a training session tutorial that included simple installation instructions as well as some examples of how to answer questions. In order to keep students motivated, we manually crafted and sent them bot-like push messages on four occasions and wrote messages on their Facebook groups. After the experiment was concluded, we asked learners to fill a survey giving them the opportunity to provide feedback on v-trel and the overall experiment.

6 Results

6.1 Participation and expertise of the crowd

Figure 1 shows the percentages of the answers provided by the 20 learners over the 17 days of the experiment, as well as the number of learners contributing every day and the moments we sent bot-like push messages to them to keep them engaged. As one can observe, the number of answers globally increased over time while the number of learners contributing fluctuated noticeably with an average of 9,2 per day (see blue bars in Figure 1). In our opinion, the overall increase of answers contributed is partly due to the prize-winning contest we organized over the first 16 days. Overall, as it can be observed in Table 1, six students contributed for 88.27% of the answers (79.79% of answers to open questions and 91.66% of answers to closed questions). We believe that the fact that our contest offered 5 vouchers, one fewer than the number of the most active learners, is no coincidence. This is a particularly interesting fact to consider for future experiments in order to maximize participation as these learners contributed voluntarily an amount of answers that most likely required between ten to twenty hours of their time, i.e., 12037 answers for the top contributor. Such an amount of time would have cost far more than a mere 20 euros voucher if we had remunerated them per hour of participation.

In Figure 1, the bot-like push messages are depicted by black stars. They mostly served their purpose as the second, third and fourth ones did induce spikes of participation whereas the first one sent after the first day wasn't very effective. From these few observations, it is fair to say that push messages seem to be a relevant tool to foster participation.

Overall, our setting allowed us to meet our goals in terms of amount of answers crowdsourced as we obtained 17108 answers to open questions (22.8 on average) and 42610 answers to closed questions (23.8 on average), which is more than twice than our original goal of obtaining an average of 10 answers per question.

With respect to the expertise, Table 1 details the overall performances of learners in answering open and closed questions computed by confronting their answers to an improved version of our gold standard for closed questions[9] and another gold standard we compiled for open questions[10]. As one can observe, despite the fact that

poral, *austrian* and *tiger mother*, which seems incorrect outside of the context that generated these relations.

[8] We originally aimed at an equivalent number of open and closed questions but a misunderstanding with the annotator that compiled the gold standard for closed questions led to the creation of a higher number of closed questions.

[9] We manually revised the entries where the strongest disagreements between the answers or the learners and the content of the gold standard could be spotted (see further details in Section 6.2).

[10] It is worth noting that the gold standard for the answers to open questions is based on a subset of the answers which are likely of being of higher accuracy in average. The performances to open questions reported are thus over estimating the true performances of the learners (see further details in

the learners are L1 Romanian speakers, their overall performances hardly qualifies them as an expert crowd for which we would have expected performances closer to the perfection (e.g. 98% accuracy)[11]. This shows that our crowd qualifies as a non-expert crowd which skills can still be improved, even though its skill-set should be noticeably above other non-expert crowds such as L2 learners.

Finally, the noticeable variability of the performances of the learners (Min / Max 69.57% / 97.56% for open questions and 58.82% / 92.12% for closed questions) confirmed our intuition that it is worth taking performances into account when aggregating their answers.

6.2 Producing expert knowledge

6.2.1 Open questions

Within the crowdsourcing workflow of v-trel, open questions are primarily meant to extend ConceptNet by collecting triples that are not encoded in it. Recurrent triples trigger the generation of closed questions that will confirm or refute their validity[12].

A single annotator performed an evaluation after the experiment on 1640 triples out of the 2513 triples[13] that had been suggested at least twice in order to create a gold standard. We then used it to study if the number of times a triple had been suggested was correlated with its quality[14]. Figure 2 demonstrates that the answer is a firm yes. Be it by considering all answers as equally important or by attributing them a weight associated with the proficiency of the learner (computed over the average accuracy of the answers of the students for the triples present in the gold standard), the quality of a triple is clearly correlated with the number of times it has been suggested. According to our evaluation, triples that were suggested with a score of 6 or more[15] were 97% correct when considering weighted votes (around 95% with regular votes).

For our use case, we can thus confirm the crowdsourcing potential of the open questions in order to produce a knowledge worth considering for extending ConceptNet.

6.2.2 Closed questions

Within the crowdsourcing workflow of v-trel, closed questions are both meant to take expert decisions to confirm or refute the triples present in ConceptNet and accept or filter out candidate triples to extend ConceptNet that have been crowdsourced in open questions. We evaluated this crowdsourcing potential in two manners.

In order to evaluate the answers to closed questions, we first confirmed that our set of closed questions did not silently induce a bias between positive and negative answers. As we collected 51.4% (21849) positive answers with an average accuracy of 83.16% and 48.6% (20665) negative ones with an average accuracy of 83.23%, there is no reason to believe that our experimental setup induced any such bias.

We first studied if the answers provided by the learners allowed to confirm or revoke the gold standard we had compiled for our experiment. In order to do so, we revisited our gold standard for all the 1972 closed questions and took into consideration how much the answers of the learners contradicted the gold answer we had associated with the closed questions. After such reconsideration, we inverted the original decision made by the single annotator that compiled the gold standard from "yes" to "no" or vice versa for 13.3% (239 questions) out of the 1792 questions and created an enhanced version of our gold standard. This confirms that, at least for our use case, the aggregated answers to closed questions crowdsourced can indeed be used to contradict the entries of a gold standard.

We then studied the quality of the winning "yes" or "no" options to the closed questions according to the minimum margin with which a winning option wins over a losing one in terms of aggregated score. Because v-trel is still a prototype that doesn't have yet an aggregation method implemented in it for closed questions, we relied on two rather simple aggregation scores: the minimum difference between a simple majority score

Section 6.2).

[11]Even though some did achieve quite respectable performances, such as the second and fourth learners.

[12]While it is not implemented in v-trel at present, open questions are also the occasion to gather positive answers for the closed questions that are automatically generated from them.

[13]We did not evaluate all 2513 that had been suggested twice or more or the other 4179 triples that had been suggested once because of manpower constraint.

[14]It is worth noting that compiling such a gold standard was only meant to double-check this correlation. Compiling a gold standard while relying on a single annotator was thus an approach of lesser quality that still met our needs.

[15]542 open questions in our gold standard met that criteria for the weighted votes and 302 for the simple votes.

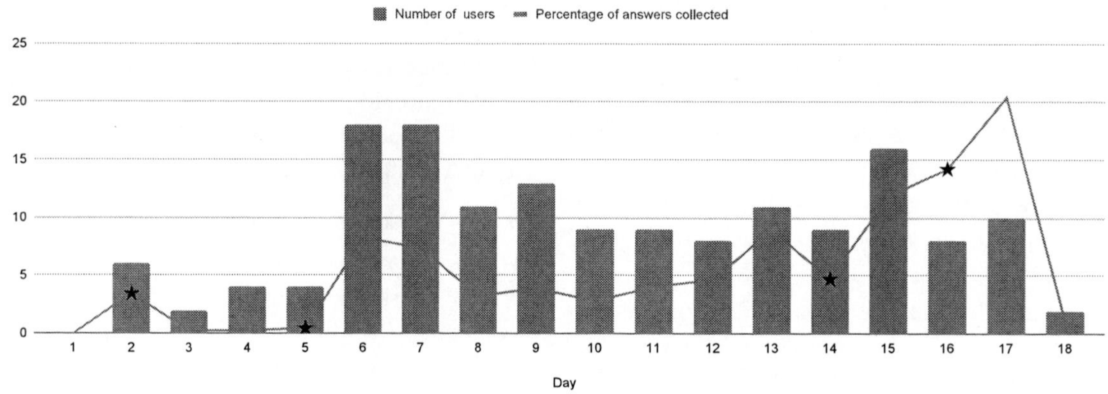

Figure 1: Percentage of the answers collected per day and numbers of contributors (stars indicate when push messages were sent)

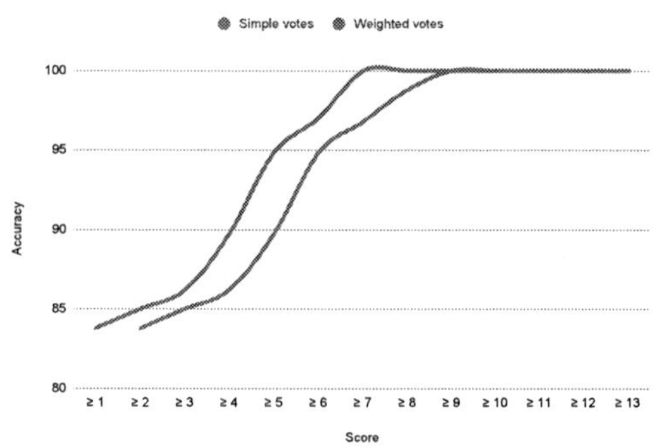

Figure 2: Accuracy of triples suggested to open question according to the number of votes.

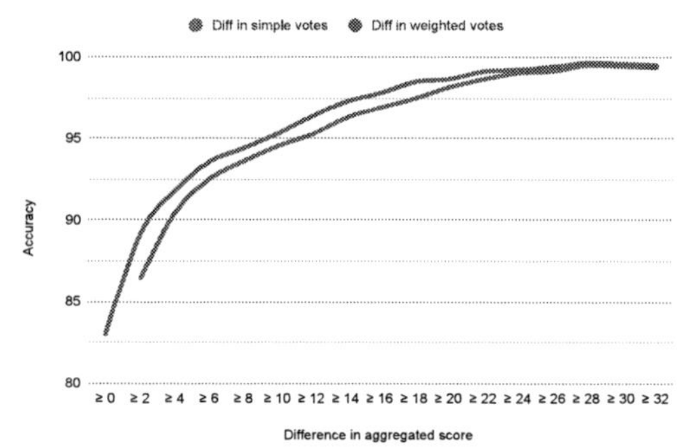

Figure 3: Accuracy of a winning option to closed questions according to the minimum difference in aggregated scores with the losing option.

and the minimum difference between a weighted majority score[16]. As can be seen in Figure 3, the greater the minimum difference between the winning option and the losing one, the higher is the accuracy of the winning option. For example, if the difference is at least of 16 points[17] then the winning option is around 98% reliable when using the weighted score, and 97% when using the simple vote[18]. This confirms once more that, at least for our use case, expert knowledge can be crowdsourced out of multiple answers provided by L1 learners to closed questions.

[16]The weight of an answer corresponded to the average accuracy of the answers of the learners according to our enhanced gold standard.

[17]639 closed questions met this criteria for the weighted scoring and 774 for the simple scoring.

[18]It should be noted that the number of answers to crowdsource for obtaining such a difference in votes depends on the triples considered.

6.3 Learning impact

In order to discuss the learning impact, we studied how the capacity of the learners in answering open and closed questions evolved over the duration of the experiment.

6.3.1 Open questions

In order to observe the learning impact regarding open questions, we reused the manual evaluation we did on the triples that were suggested at least twice by learners (see Section 6.2) and computed an average accuracy for their first 750 answers.

The reason why we only considered this set of answers is due to the fact that we had prepared 750 open questions and, since some learners provided more than 750 answers, they answered some questions several times. And when the learners were confronted with a question they had already answered, they were requested to provide an answer

Id	School	All questions		Open questions				Closed questions			
		#	% answers	#	% answers	Acc	# evals	#	% answers	Acc	# evals
1	1	12037	20.16	2821	16.49	89.66	774	9216	21.63	80.2	9190
2	2	9600	16.08	1921	11.23	88.15	852	7679	18.02	92.12	7669
3	1	9207	15.42	2023	11.82	86.2	1065	7184	16.86	87.82	7158
4	1	8589	14.38	2300	13.44	87.91	951	6289	14.76	90	6273
5	2	7994	13.39	2101	12.28	85.39	1437	5893	13.83	71.79	5880
6	2	5280	8.84	2486	14.53	85.94	1330	2794	6.56	76.81	2786
7	2	2067	3.46	1021	5.97	88.91	487	1046	2.45	75.69	1045
8	2	1070	1.79	512	2.99	79.75	237	558	1.31	74.64	556
9	1	1033	1.73	541	3.16	96.25	267	492	1.15	67.68	492
10	2	544	0.91	256	1.5	97.56	41	288	0.68	61.11	288
11	2	472	0.79	232	1.36	87.4	127	240	0.56	78.66	239
12	2	397	0.66	195	1.14	84.54	97	202	0.47	81.09	201
13	2	297	0.5	147	0.86	-	-	150	0.35	80	150
14	2	259	0.43	128	0.75	95.7	93	131	0.31	87.02	131
15	1	254	0.43	125	0.73	87.32	71	129	0.3	82.03	128
16	2	182	0.3	88	0.51	-	-	94	0.22	69.15	94
17	2	140	0.23	69	0.4	75	16	71	0.17	83.1	71
18	1	102	0.17	48	0.28	90	30	54	0.13	81.48	54
19	2	99	0.17	48	0.28	-	-	51	0.12	58.82	51
20	1	95	0.16	46	0.27	69.57	23	49	0.11	77.08	48

Table 1: Number, percentage of answers provided and accuracy of answers per learner and per type of exercises (*# evals* indicate the number of answers that matched a question in our gold standards).

different from the ones already provided. The difficulty of a question was thus increasing every time it came back. Another aspect that negatively impacted the quality of answers to questions coming back is that we did not offer them the opportunity to skip an open question. By doing so, we forced them to provide answers, including suboptimal ones, in order to be allowed to move forward. For all these reasons, observing the evolution of the performances of learners to open questions can only be performed soundly on the first 750 answers.

The average accuracy of the subset of theses answers that had an entry in our gold standard are shown in Figure 4. As one can observe, they remained globally stable around 90% over this set of 750 answers and no progress can be observed. This is unfortunately due to another bias that this experiment allowed us to identify. Indeed, as explained earlier in Section 6.2, the more often an answer to an open questions occurs the more likely it is to be correct. As such, by not considering the answers that occurred only once and were thus not included in our gold standard, we just keep on evaluating a subset of answers for which the quality is stable over the time span of the experiment. In order to perform this evaluation, we would have needed to have a gold standard for the whole set of the first 750 answers of each of the learners and not a subset of the best ones. The increased quality of the answers can nonetheless be observed in an indirect fashion by observing the ratio over time of answers matching an entry of our gold standard vs the answers not matching any entry (that are overall of lesser quality). As observable in Figure 4, this ratio increased over time, which indirectly indicates that the accuracy of the answers provided increased, even though we can't evaluate directly to what extent.

The learning impact for open questions could thus be indirectly observed. Nonetheless, because of the many issues we listed above, its evaluation remains a subject we would need to address more conclusively in future work (see Section 7).

6.3.2 Closed questions

In order to observe the learning impact for closed questions, and instead of doing pre- and post-tests on the learner to observe the differences in performances before and after using v-trel, we chose to study the evolution of the performances of the learners over time with the idea in mind that the first and last set of answers can be seen as a form of pre- and post-tests. Figure 5 displays the average accuracy for sets of 250 answers ordered in time for the eight learners that provided more than 500 answers to the closed questions. As one can observe, the curves fluctuate greatly and do not have

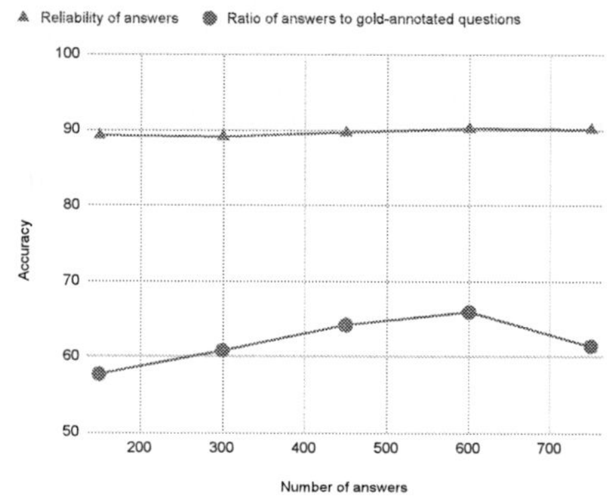

Figure 4: Accuracy and ratio of the first 750 answers to gold-annotated open questions.

the increasing direction we would have expected, with many of the curves stagnating and some even dropping. Table 2 displays for the eight learners the average accuracy of the first two hundred fifty answers, the first half of the overall answers, the second half of them and the last two hundred fifty answers provided. In that case also, our original expectations of a greater quality for the second half of the answers were not always met, with four learners performing better over time, two performing similarly and two performing worse.

We also could observe that despite using a first and last set of answers of rather large size (250 answers), the observations we could deduce regarding the learning impact on the learners from their accuracy would not always match the ones we would deduce from observing the accuracy of the larger sets consisting in the first and second half of all answers. For example, evaluating the learning impact from the first and the last sets of 250 answers or the first and second half of all answers would have led us to different conclusions for the first three learners listed in Table 2.

The fact that the four learners whose performances stagnated or decreased during the second half of their participation were part of the group that won a prize for their participation leads us to suspect that the competition among them might have had a deterring effect on the quality of their answers. We thus suspect that the strategy to earn points for these learners was to favor quantity over quality (i.e. speed over reflection). The fact that more than half of the answers were provided during the last four days of the experiment would tend to confirm our intuition (see Figure 1). If our intuition is indeed correct, while we had foreseen that such a phenomenon could happen, we underestimated its extent. In the event that we run another experiment that includes such a contest, we would need to devise strategies to prevent such a side-effect (see Section 7).

Overall, the learning impact for closed questions could not clearly be confirmed for many learners. At the same time, we could not think of, or observe, any intrinsic reason why there wouldn't be one for all learners. Confirming the learning impact of closed questions thus remains an open question to address.

6.4 User feedback

With respect to user feedback, 10 learners filled the post-experiment survey asking them questions with a free text, boolean or Likert format. During the survey, the learners were asked their thoughts on open and closed questions (free text), as well as the usefulness of these questions in vocabulary training (boolean), and the ratio of open and closed questions they prefer (Likert scale). The learners were also asked with two Likert scales how much they used the "hint" functionality and the automatically generated Wikipedia links (see Section 3) and how useful they thought it was (boolean), as well as whether they had any feedback about it (free text). They were finally asked about their overall user experience with the vocabulary trainer (Likert scale), what they liked and didn't like (free text), their thoughts on the Telegram interface and if they had any additional feedback (free text).

The students mostly gave positive feedback on the open questions, and two of them pointed out an important aspect of the Romanian language, namely the polysemy of words, which can be difficult to differentiate between the meanings of two words written identically in the absence of diacritics. All survey participants that gave a free response to the question about their thoughts on the closed questions mostly listed how simple the questions seemed at first glance, but that they took time to think of an answer. They offered a positive feedback regarding the usefulness of both types of questions for training vocabulary. Seven out of the ten survey's participants showed a preference for open questions over the closed questions.

Regarding the "hint" functionality, seven of the participants said they used it for less than half of the questions, while the rest said they used it for

User	First 250	First half	Second half	Last 250	Progress
1	84.4	84.26	76.13	93.12	worse
2	80	92.2	92.05	93.6	similar
3	88.4	88.23	87.4	80.4	similar
4	78	87.66	92.35	90.4	better
5	76.8	75.57	68	67.2	worse
6	70	74.35	79.27	81.2	better
7	54.4	68.97	82.41	80	better
8	70.8	71.48	77.78	78.4	better

Table 2: Accuracy of the answers of learners to closed questions for the first two hundred fifty, the first half, the second half and the last two hundred fifty of their answers.

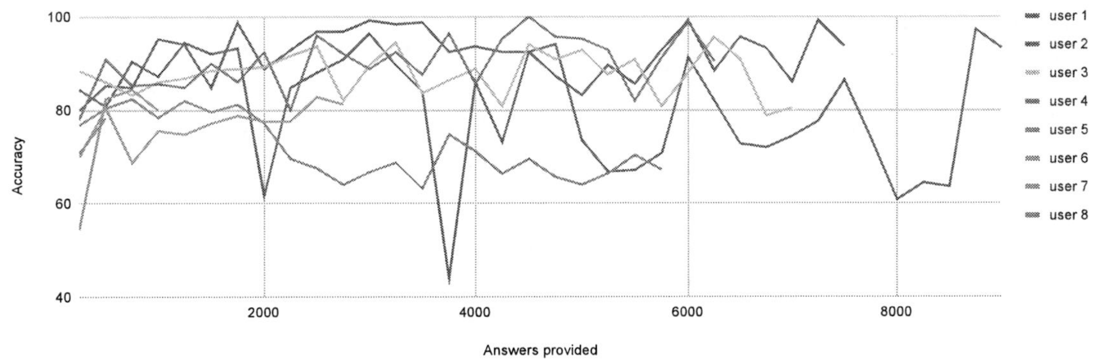

Figure 5: Average quality of the answers to closed questions over time by sets of 250 answers.

almost half of them. When asked about its usefulness, all the users found it useful. When asked about the Wikipedia links, students indicated that the links do not always correspond to the word in question or can lead to a non-existent page. Nonetheless, nine out of ten participants believed that the Wikipedia links are effective.

The participants' feedback about how much the trainer helped them to improve their vocabulary was rather positive, 8 out of 10 said that the game helped them "a lot" and the rest of them said that the game helped them to some degree. When asked about the difficulty of the words used with which they were trained, none of them considered them "too difficult", six of the participants considered them "neither too easy nor too difficult", and the four others as "mostly easy".

With respect to user experience, the vocabulary trainer seems to have met the expectations of the participants of the survey, who all indicated that it was fun to use. We can conclude that the instructions given prior to the start of the game were helpful because none of the participants expressed concern about the game being confusing or frustrating to play. Also two of the ten participants said that it was inspiring using the vocabulary trainer. When asked what they liked or disliked about this approach, the participants stated that they had a pleasant insight with the vocabulary teaching approach, and that while playing, their vocabulary skills improved. They also indicated that the competition and prizes influenced their involvement during this period. Regarding the Telegram chatbot interface, the learners claimed that they had a pleasant interaction with it. Just one person raised a concern about its instability on some occasions.

Last but not least, with respect to additional feedback, some students took the occasion to thank us for the opportunity. One student also mentioned that despite having enjoyed the game, he believed that it was better suited to middle school students.

7 Future work

Despite being satisfied with part of our results, this experiment allowed us to discover a set of shortcomings in the way we approached the experiment, on top of the challenges that we had already reported in earlier publications and that were addressed in this experiment.

Regarding the crowdsourcing potential of v-trel, we now have a dataset of real answers to closed question from learners and a refined gold standard dataset allowing us to know if the answers were correct or incorrect. As such, we have the data needed to start testing aggregation methods that could be included in v-trel. Another aspect we would like to further explore with respect to the crowdsourcing potential is to confirm its validity for other use cases relying on another type of semantic relation (e.g. hyponymy or hypernymy), for a different type of crowd or for a different language. By doing so, we would be able to see if any specific issues arise and how much our current conclusions can be extrapolated or generalized.

Regarding the learning impact, we first and foremost need to evaluate it in a more convincing fashion for both the open and closed questions. That would imply addressing the shortcomings listed in Section 6.3. For open questions, we would need to perform the post-experiment manual evaluation to build a gold standard either on the whole set of answers or a randomly picked subset. We would need to allow learners to skip questions if they have no convincing answers and would need to find means to consider all answers of learners and not only the first ones to each question. It would also be interesting to observe the learning impact for other use cases and see once again how the new results compare to the ones we obtained from this experiment. Furthermore, it would as well be interesting to compare v-trel to an equivalent solution such as the vocabulary trainers available on existing language learning solutions. However such a comparison is difficult to perform empirically on the performances of learners as it would require, first, to involve two crowds of learners that are large enough in order to ensure that any results computed are statistically relevant, second, that the two crowds are similar in terms of learners profiles in order to ensure that a tool doesn't have a more favorable crowd than the other and third, that both crowds contribute a similar amount of time. All in all, comparing v-trel to an equivalent solution in a relevant and meaningful fashion is a challenge that we do not know yet how to tackle.

Be it in terms of crowdsourcing potential or learning impact, it would be interesting to explore to which extent our results and conclusions also apply to L2 learners. Indeed, if we consider that the skills regarding language, including a mother-tongue, are a continuum, then L1 learners are among the most capable non-expert crowds we could rely on. We suspect that relying on L2 learners would not make a noticeable difference with the exception that the answers will be of lesser quality, which would certainly require us to adapt our approach to some extent.

Finally, if we were to also organize a contest to win prizes to foster participation in a future experiment, we would need to find means to mitigate the noise that we suspect such competition creates by encouraging learners to favor speed over reflection. A simple strategy could be to award an always greater amount of points for series of consecutive correct answers.

8 Conclusion

In this paper, we presented an experiment performed with the aim of evaluating if knowledge of expert quality about Romanian synonyms could be crowdsourced from language learners. Such an evaluation aimed at confirming the viability of a fully learner-fueled crowdsourcing workflow for improving such type of linguistic resources.

To perform such an experiment, we adapted an existing open-source crowdsourcing vocabulary trainer called v-trel that we designed for this very purpose. Our results clearly confirmed that such expert knowledge could indeed be produced by relying on L1 language learners and that v-trel would be a suitable tool to produce it, once some missing pieces regarding the aggregation of answers and the automatic generation of closed questions would be completed. The practical experience we obtained while running this experiment reinforced our intuition that expert knowledge about semantic relations between words other than synonymy could also be produced in an similar fashion.

We also took the occasion to further investigate the learning impact of v-trel on learners. On this subject our observations are far less conclusive. On the one hand, while we do believe that there has been a learning impact overall, our data does not allow us to draw any clear conclusions on this subject for all learners. On the other hand, we observed clear shortcomings in the way we evaluated the open questions and, with respect to closed questions, we suspect that the contest to win rewards has had a deterring effect on the quality of the answers provided. In order to demonstrate the learning impact of v-trel, we thus need to first address these two issues in a follow-up experiment.

Acknowledgements. We would like to thank *Constantin Hoţoleanu* and *Daniela Pavel* from the *Liceul Teoretic Emil Racoviţă Vaslui* and the *Colegiul Tehnic Ion Creangă Târgu Neamţ* for supporting us in performing this experiment. This article is based upon work from COST Action enetCollect (CA16105), supported by COST (European Cooperation in Science and Technology).

References

Luis von Ahn. 2013. Duolingo: Learn a language for free while helping to translate the web. In *Proceedings of the 2013 International Conference on Intelligent User Interfaces*, IUI '13, page 1–2, New York, NY, USA. Association for Computing Machinery.

David Alfter, Elena Volodina, Lars Borin, Ildikó Pilan, and Herbert Lange. 2019. Proceedings of the 8th workshop on nlp for computer assisted language learning. In *Proceedings of the 8th Workshop on NLP for Computer Assisted Language Learning*.

Špela Arhar Holdt, Nataša Logar, Eva Pori, and Iztok Kosem. 2021. "Game of Words": Play the Game, Clean the Database. In *Proceedings of the 14th Congress of the European Association for Lexicography (EURALEX 2021)*, pages 41–49, Alexandroupolis, Greece.

Andrew Caines, Christian Bentz, Calbert Graham, Tim Polzehl, and Paula Buttery. 2016. Crowdsourcing a multi-lingual speech corpus: Recording, transcription and annotation of the crowdis corpora. In *Proceedings of the Tenth International Conference on Language Resources and Evaluation (LREC'16)*, pages 2145–2152.

Maria Chinkina, Simón Ruiz, and Detmar Meurers. 2017. Automatically generating questions to support the acquisition of particle verbs: evaluating via crowdsourcing. *CALL in a climate of change: adapting to turbulent global conditions*, page 73.

Maria Chinkina, Simón Ruiz, and Detmar Meurers. 2020. Crowdsourcing evaluation of the quality of automatically generated questions for supporting computer-assisted language teaching. *ReCALL*, 32(2):145–161.

Kordula De Kuthy, Madeeswaran Kannan, Haemanth Santhi Ponnusamy, and Detmar Meurers. 2020. Towards automatically generating questions under discussion to link information and discourse structure. In *Proceedings of the 28th International Conference on Computational Linguistics*, pages 5786–5798.

Alena Fenogenova and Elizaveta Kuzmenko. 2016. Automatic generation of lexical exercises. In *Proceedings of the International Conference*.

Amarsanaa Ganbold, Altangerel Chagnaa, and Gábor Bella. 2018. Using crowd agreement for wordnet localization. In *Proceedings of the Eleventh International Conference on Language Resources and Evaluation (LREC 2018)*.

Marianne Grace Araneta, Gülsen Eryigit, Alexander König, Ji-Ung Lee, Ana Luís, Verena Lyding, Lionel Nicolas, Christos Rodosthenous, and Federico Sangati. 2020. Substituto - A Synchronous Educational Language Game for Simultaneous Teaching and Crowdsourcing. In *Proceedings of the 9th Workshop on Natural Language Processing for Computer Assisted Language Learning (NLP4CALL 2020)*, pages 1–9.

Bruno Guillaume, Karën Fort, and Nicolas Lefebvre. 2016. Crowdsourcing complex language resources: Playing to annotate dependency syntax. In *Proceedings of COLING 2016, the 26th International Conference on Computational Linguistics: Technical Papers*, pages 3041–3052, Osaka, Japan. The COLING 2016 Organizing Committee.

Jennifer Hill and Rahul Simha. 2016. Automatic generation of context-based fill-in-the-blank exercises using co-occurrence likelihoods and Google n-grams. In *Proceedings of the 11th Workshop on Innovative Use of NLP for Building Educational Applications*, pages 23–30, San Diego, CA. Association for Computational Linguistics.

Barbora Hladká, Jirka Hana, and Ivana Lukšová. 2014. Crowdsourcing in language classes can help natural language processing. In *Proceedings of the AAAI Conference on Human Computation and Crowdsourcing*, volume 2.

Valia Kordoni, Antal van den Bosch, Katia Lida Kermanidis, Vilelmini Sosoni, Kostadin Cholakov, Iris Hendrickx, Matthias Huck, and Andy Way. 2016. Enhancing access to online education: Quality machine translation of MOOC content. In *Proceedings of the Tenth International Conference on Language Resources and Evaluation (LREC'16)*, pages 16–22, Portorož, Slovenia. European Language Resources Association (ELRA).

Mathieu Lafourcade. 2007. Making people play for lexical acquisition with the jeuxdemots prototype. In *SNLP'07: 7th international symposium on natural language processing*, page 7.

Ji-Ung Lee, Erik Schwan, and Christian M Meyer. 2019. Manipulating the difficulty of c-tests. *arXiv preprint arXiv:1906.06905*.

Verena Lyding, Christos Rodosthenous, Federico Sangati, Umair ul Hassan, Lionel Nicolas, Alexander König, Jolita Horbacauskiene, and Anisia Katinskaia. 2019. v-trel: Vocabulary trainer for tracing word relations-an implicit crowdsourcing approach. In *Proceedings of the International Conference on Recent Advances in Natural Language Processing (RANLP 2019)*, pages 674–683.

Alice Millour, Marianne Grace Araneta, Ivana Lazić Konjik, Annalisa Raffone, Yann-Alan Pilatte, and Karën Fort. 2019. Katana and Grand Guru: a Game of the Lost Words (DEMO). In *Proceedings of the ninth Language & Technology Conference*, Poznan, Poland.

Lionel Nicolas, Verena Lyding, Claudia Borg, Corina Forascu, Karën Fort, Katerina Zdravkova, Iztok Kosem, Jaka Čibej, Špela Arhar Holdt, Alice Millour, Alexander König, Christos Rodosthenous, Federico Sangati, Umair ul Hassan, Anisia Katinskaia, Anabela Barreiro, Lavinia Aparaschivei, and Yaakov HaCohen-Kerner. 2020. Creating expert knowledge by relying on language learners: a generic approach for mass-producing language resources by combining implicit crowdsourcing and language learning. In *Proceedings of the 12th Language Resources and Evaluation Conference*, pages 268–278, Marseille, France. European Language Resources Association.

Massimo Poesio, Jon Chamberlain, Udo Kruschwitz, Livio Robaldo, and Luca Ducceschi. 2013. Phrase detectives: Utilizing collective intelligence for internet-scale language resource creation. *ACM Transactions on Interactive Intelligent Systems (TiiS)*, 3(1):1–44.

Matt Post, Chris Callison-Burch, and Miles Osborne. 2012. Constructing parallel corpora for six indian languages via crowdsourcing. In *Proceedings of the Seventh Workshop on Statistical Machine Translation*, pages 401–409.

Christos Rodosthenous, Verena Lyding, Federico Sangati, Alexander König, Umair ul Hassan, Lionel Nicolas, Jolita Horbacauskiene, Anisia Katinskaia, and Lavinia Aparaschivei. 2020. Using crowdsourced exercises for vocabulary training to expand conceptnet. In *Proceedings of The 12th Language Resources and Evaluation Conference*, pages 307–316.

Christos T. Rodosthenous, Verena Lyding, Alexander König, Jolita Horbacauskiene, Anisia Katinskaia, Umair ul Hassan, Nicos Isaak, Federico Sangati, and Lionel Nicolas. 2019. Designing a prototype architecture for crowdsourcing language resources. In *Proceedings of the Poster Session of the 2nd Conference on Language, Data and Knowledge (LDK 2019), Leipzig, Germany, May 21, 2019*, volume 2402 of *CEUR Workshop Proceedings*, pages 17–23. CEUR-WS.org.

Federico Sangati, Stefano Merlo, and Giovanni Moretti. 2015. School-tagging: interactive language exercises in classrooms. In *LTLT@ SLaTE*, pages 16–19.

Pavel Smrz. 2019. Crowdsourcing Complex Associations among Words by Means of A Game. In *Proceedings of CSTY 2019, 5th International Conference on Computer Science and Information Technology.*, volume 9, Dubai, UAE.

Robyn Speer, Joshua Chin, and Catherine Havasi. 2017. Conceptnet 5.5: An open multilingual graph of general knowledge. In *Proceedings of the Thirty-First AAAI Conference on Artificial Intelligence*, AAAI'17, page 4444–4451. AAAI Press.

Joel Tetreault, Jill Burstein, Ekaterina Kochmar, Claudia Leacock, and Helen Yannakoudakis. 2018. Proceedings of the thirteenth workshop on innovative use of nlp for building educational applications. In *Proceedings of the Thirteenth Workshop on Innovative Use of NLP for Building Educational Applications*.

Nicole Ziegler, Detmar Meurers, Patrick Rebuschat, Simon Ruiz, José L Moreno-Vega, Maria Chinkina, Wenjing Li, and Sarah Grey. 2017. Interdisciplinary research at the intersection of call, nlp, and sla: Methodological implications from an input enhancement project. *Language Learning*, 67(S1):209–231.

Automatic annotation of curricular language targets to enrich activity models and support both pedagogy and adaptive systems

Martí Quixal[1,2,3] **Björn Rudzewitz**[1,2] **Elizabeth Bear**[1,4] **Detmar Meurers**[1,2]

[1]Department of Linguistics, University of Tübingen, Germany
[2]LEAD Graduate School and Research Network, University of Tübingen, Germany
[3]Department of School Psychology, University of Tübingen, Germany
[4]Hector Research Institute of Education Sciences and Psychology, University of Tübingen, Germany

marti.quixal@psycho.uni-tuebingen.de, br@sfs.uni-tuebingen.de, elizabeth.bear@uni-tuebingen.de, dm@sfs.uni-tuebingen.de

Abstract

Integrating an adaptive Intelligent Tutoring System (ITS) in real-life school contexts requires coverage of the official curricula, which necessitates a broad range and number of activities to practice the official set of language phenomena. In the context of developing an adaptive ITS for English as a Foreign Language, we propose a method to automatically derive rich activity models from ordinary exercise specifications. The method identifies the language means being covered from the curriculum by processing the language used in the exercise and exemplary answers.

The analysis serves two purposes: First, it informs material developers about the extent to which the materials appropriately cover the language means to be practiced according to the curriculum. Second, it helps establish a direct link between rich activity and learner models, as needed for adaptively sequencing activities.

The approach includes (1) an NLP-based information extraction module annotating language means using a pedagogically-informed categorization, and (2) a tool to generate activity models offering information on the language properties of each activity in quantitative, qualitative, specific or aggregated terms. We exemplify the benefits of the method proposed in the design of materials for an ITS for language learning used in school.

1 Introduction

Foreign language teaching and learning in schools is typically regulated by education policy makers in state or national curricula that define which language aspects should be mastered in which grade. The curricula guide the creation of learning materials and textbooks, with publishing houses developing the materials for each grade, often followed by a government authority confirming whether the material appropriately covers the curriculum.

While the curriculum characterizes the envisioned language learning goals, teachers know that every student learns and makes progress in different ways. The substantial heterogeneity of classes in principle requires differentiation strategies that cater to the diverse learning paces and processes (Tomlinson, 2015), a highly non-trivial task (Martin-Beltrán et al., 2017). Instruction strategies supported by Intelligent Tutoring Systems (ITSs) have been shown to be effective, with most approaches targeting STEM subjects (Ma et al., 2014; VanLehn, 2011), but some recent work also focusing on foreign language learning (Choi, 2016; Meurers et al., 2019).

Complementing face-to-face instruction with ITSs makes it possible to support individual language learners by allowing them to practice with scaffolding feedback (Meurers et al., 2019). In addition, adaptive ITSs can select and sequence activities based on their difficulty in relation to the learner's knowledge and the learning goal, which presupposes the existence of both an activity and a learner model.

In this paper, we introduce an approach that facilitates the automatic derivation of activity models that can be used to assess curriculum compliance and support individual learning sequences in line with the principles of instructed Second Language Acquisition (Loewen and Sato, 2017).

Martí Quixal, Björn Rudzewitz, Elizabeth Bear and Detmar Meurers 2021. Automatic annotation of curricular language targets to enrich activity models and support both pedagogy and adaptive systems. *Proceedings of the 10th Workshop on Natural Language Processing for Computer Assisted Language Learning (NLP4CALL 2021)*. Linköping Electronic Conference Proceedings 177: 15–27.

SuperCategory	SubCategory	Level	Can-do statement
PRESENT	present simple	A1	FORM: NEGATIVE Can use the negative form with a limited range of regular and irregular verbs.
PRESENT	present continuous	A1	FORM: AFFIRMATIVE Can use the affirmative form.
PRESENT	present simple	A1	USE: HABITS AND GENERAL FACTS Can use the present simple to talk about repeated events or habits, and general facts.

Figure 1: EGP example descriptors for grammatical accuracy for CEFR A1 level

After introducing related work on identifying language phenomena in learner language and in activity models in section 2, we describe the implementation context of our approach and the resources developed in section 3. We then present and exemplify the process of generating activity models in section 4, showcase the application of the approach in the educational context in terms of curriculum coverage and ITS development in section 5, and conclude with a discussion of limitations and future work.

2 Related work

Learning a foreign language requires being exposed to, practicing and producing the language in question (Gass and Mackey, 2013). A range of pedagogical techniques are designed to engage learners in functionally using language, and a balance between fluency and accuracy as well as between receptive and productive skills is sought (Brown, 2007). Integrating ITSs in a school context has the potential advantage of enabling teachers to focus on the communicative aspects of language in the classroom, while the system supports individualized learning of grammar, vocabulary, listening and reading skills – aspects where individual differences also play an important role (Dörnyei and Skehan, 2003).

The definition of fine-grained foreign language curricula including a formal specification of language structures based on communicative goals is an endeavor argued for by modern approaches to language instruction (Estaire and Zanón, 1994; Bachman and Palmer, 1996). However, the link between the communicative goals and the linguistic syllabus is rarely made explicit in practice.

In an effort to spell out aspects of the CEFR linguistic competence scales (Council of Europe, 2020, p. 130), the English Grammar Profile (EGP) Project[1] and Pearson's Global Scale of English[2] have compiled databases linking can-do statements to vocabulary and grammar structures. They include detailed information on the linguistic structures as well as the mastery levels at which such structures are produced (not just taught).

The EGP organizes its inventory based on 19 super-categories[3] (from *adjectives* to *verbs* over *adverbs*, *clauses*, etc.), with up to ten sub-categories each (e.g., for the super-category *present*, the sub-categories are *simple* and *continuous*). For each sub-category, a number of level-specific can-do statements is provided. Figure 1 illustrates the first three items for the super-category *present (tenses)* for the CEFR level A1, including both form and functional use characterizations.

The EGP is designed to help analyze and evaluate learner productions. To analyze teaching materials, verify curriculum coverage and generate activity models supporting adaptive selection and sequencing in an ITS, we need to go a step further and analyze the language in the input given that it "[i]s an essential component for learning in that it provides the crucial evidence from which learners can form linguistic hypotheses" (Gass and Mackey, 2015). When considering practice, we need to analyze the learner activities to determine which language students are expected to produce.

The few language tutoring systems that so far have been developed and used in real-life contexts (Heift, 2010; Nagata, 2009; Amaral and Meurers, 2011; Choi, 2016; Ziai et al., 2018) are based on manual activity specifications and do not provide a fine-grained characterization of the language means they cover. While some research tackles the task of automatically annotating texts with lin-

[1] https://englishprofile.org/english-grammar-profile
[2] https://english.com/gse/teacher-toolkit/user/grammar
[3] https://englishprofile.org/english-grammar-profile/grammatical-categories

guistic properties to support language-aware document retrieval (Chinkina and Meurers, 2016) or input enrichment and enhancement (Meurers et al., 2010), the work so far fell short of generating tutoring system activities that are pedagogically linked to a linguistic syllabus or curriculum.

The approach we are presenting in this paper goes a step further in automatically deriving fine-grained metalinguistic characterizations of the language used in or elicited by some given learning material, including both the linguistic phenomena targeted by the materials as well as those incidentally occurring in it.

3 Implementation context and resources

The research presented here is being carried out in the context of the development of Didi (http://didi.schule), an adaptive ITS for English as a Foreign Language based on the FeedBook system (Rudzewitz et al., 2017; Meurers et al., 2018). It integrates the feedback mechanisms from FeedBook and offers immediate, specific feedback on grammar (Rudzewitz et al., 2018), spelling (Ziai et al., 2019), and meaning (Ziai et al., 2018). Instead of offering exercises from an existing workbook, the Didi system provides independent exercises on more diverse levels of difficulty.

The minimal components of an ITS, such as Didi or FeedBook, are illustrated in Figure 2.

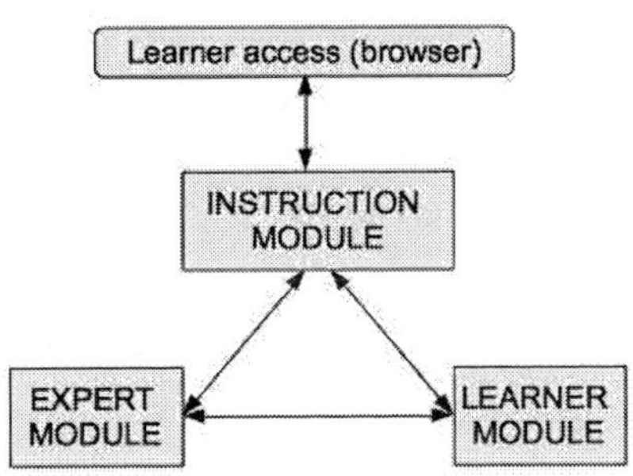

Figure 2: ITS architecture (adapted from Amaral, 2007, p. 85)

The method we present aims at using the linguistic structures identified in a given set of learning activities to link (i) language as an object of study (language as a system), which belongs to the expert module, (ii) language as organized and presented in instruction materials (language as a pedagogical goal), which is part of the instruction module, and (iii) language as knowledge that has been or is being acquired, which is part of the learner module (language as a competence). The three perspectives on language need to be anchored in a common characterization of language properties supporting the goals of the three modules of an ITS.

Our approach makes it possible to automatically populate the knowledge domain as part of the expert module on the basis of the language properties of the activities in the instruction module. The knowledge domain results as an aggregate of all the linguistic constructions found in the activities produced by material authors and organized as learning sequences. As we will see in section 5, it also allows us to monitor and make explicit learner competencies by enriching the learner model and ultimately perform adaptive sequencing.

As a starting point, we describe three resources that facilitate the automatization of this process: (i) a hierarchical structure of language phenomena relevant for English as a Foreign Language, (ii) a general linguistic annotation module, and (iii) a rule-based module for the annotation of language structures.

3.1 Knowledge hierarchy

The English as a Foreign Language (domain) knowledge of our ITS is organized as a hierarchy that consists of three levels of characterization exemplified in Figure 3. The first level includes categories such as word formation (morphology), sentence structure (syntax) and language use, levels of linguistic description common in Second Language Acquisition and Foreign Language Instruction. Each of these categories is in turn divided into smaller categories extracted and/or extended from the official curriculum for secondary schools, grades 7 to 9 (Kultusministerium, 2016, p. 50), which is the second level of characterization. This second level of characterization is exemplified in Figure 3 with superlative forms of adjectives, child nodes of the category word formation: regular forms (*reg. forms*), irregular forms (*irreg. forms*) and periphrastic forms (*most* + ADJ).

This third level of characterization is extracted or extended from the EGP, and it maps to level 2 categories so that each level 3 element relates to one and only one level 2 element. In Figure 3 this is exemplified with finer-grained labels for language means that are child nodes of the level 2 element *Superlative regular forms*: plain regular forms (*cheap - cheapest*), regular forms of ad-

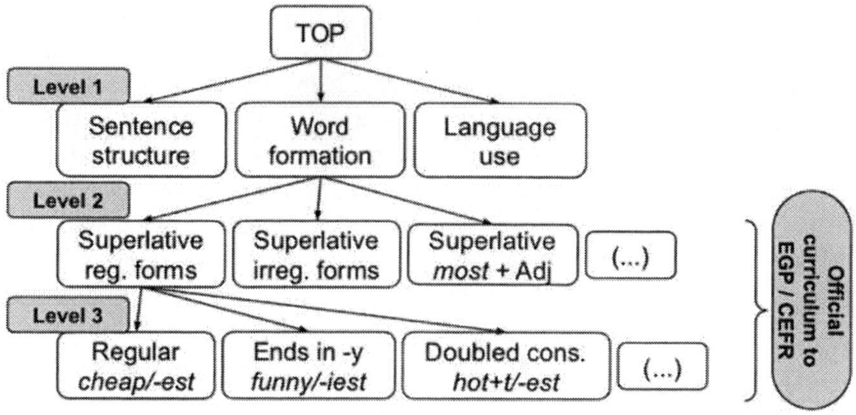

Figure 3: Hierarchical knowledge structure for English as a Foreign Language.

jectives ending in *-y* (*funny - funniest*) and regular forms ending in *-e* (*nice - nicest*). Moreover, the language means in level 3 constitute the specifications for the automatic analysis with the rule-based annotation tool.

3.2 Linguistic annotation

As we will describe in further detail in the following section, the input to the annotation module is the set of activities included in Didi.

The NLP analysis is realized in the Unstructured Information Management Architecture (UIMA, Ferrucci and Lally, 2004). As the first step, each language learning exercise provided as input is turned into a UIMA Common Analysis Structure (CAS) object. These CAS objects are linguistically annotated using the standard NLP tools specified in Table 1. Then the annotated CAS documents are exported as XMI files, the input format for the module responsible for the annotation of language means.

3.3 Annotation of language means

The module for the annotation of language means is implemented as a set of rule-based grammars in UIMA Ruta (Kluegl et al., 2016), a formalism and annotator development environment within UIMA that supports the robust and modular integration of this functionality in the processing pipeline. UIMA Ruta enables grammar writers to access annotations in the CAS that were provided by the NLP analysis modules and offers a set of operators and property check functions to map, review and remove annotations at the word, phrase, clause, sentence and document level.

Figure 4 exemplifies a UIMA Ruta rule that

NLP task	tool
segmentation	ClearNLP (Choi and Palmer, 2012)
part-of-speech (POS) tagging	ClearNLP
dependency parsing	ClearNLP
lemmatization	Morpha (Minnen et al., 2001)
morphological analysis	Sfst (Schmid, 2005)

Table 1: NLP tools adding linguistic annotations as input to UIMA Ruta

checks for the presence of a simple present tense form and, when found, records that there is a present simple verb form in terms of word formation and, in terms of sentence structure, that we are dealing with an affirmative sentence in the present. It thereby translates the NLP analysis output into two labels of level 3 in our knowledge hierarchy of English as a Foreign Language, namely "PresentSimpleForms" and "SyntAffirmativeSentencePresentSimple".

Currently the annotation module contains more than 200 rules. The module includes annotators for tenses (including present, past and future verb forms), comparatives (including comparatives and superlatives), passive voice, conditional sentences types 1 and 2, and relative clauses.

4 Generation of activity models

Activity models, which belong to the instruction module of an ITS, are particularly important for

```
(#)(NC)(ADV?)(Tense{REGEXP(Tense.value,"SIMPLE_PRESENT")})
(# (PERIOD|EXCLAMATION)){ ->
    CREATE(Construct,4,4,"constructName"="PresentSimpleForms"),
    CREATE(Construct,1,5,"constructName"="SyntAffirmativeSentencePresentSimple")};
```

Figure 4: UIMA Ruta rule to annotate present verb forms and affirmative sentences.

supporting adaptive selection and sequencing of activities for a given user since they make explicit what the activity demands and offers.

Figure 5 shows the information included in our activity model. The first block shows the specifications provided manually during activity creation. The second block, shown in italics, lists the type of information added automatically using the NLP-based and other activity-specification-based annotation modules.

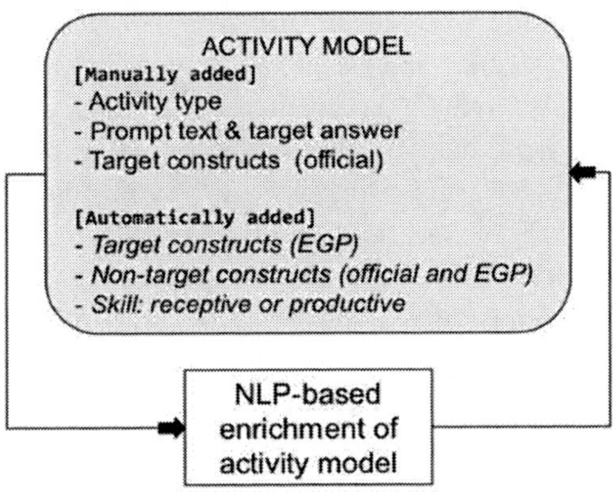

Figure 5: Linguistic enrichment of activity model

The manually determined properties include the activity's format (fill-in-the-blanks, multiple choice, etc.), the actual items, each including a prompt (textual or not), an expected answer (which may be typed in or selected), and optionally distractors. Among them there is also the learning goal, which maps to the level 2 language phenomena introduced in section 3.1 for which the activity has been designed. These phenomena become then language target (the target is to teach or learn them), as opposed to other language means, which are just accompanying the target of the activities – thus, non-target.

The automatically generated properties include language targets of level 3, and non-targets of level 2 and level 3. Non-target means are language elements present in the activities with which a specific language structure is to be practiced, but they do not belong together. For instance, to learn the use of comparatives, one needs to be able to produce sentences with them; therefore, a learner has to be able to use some sentence structure (e.g., basic SVO) and at least one tense form (e.g., the present simple).

The activity model also encodes the distinction between receptive and productive skills, which is computed on the basis of the activity's format, not its linguistic characteristics.

4.1 Input to NLP module

To illustrate the process, let us take a look at two sample activities with slightly different properties. Figure 6 shows part of a fill-in-the-blanks activity.

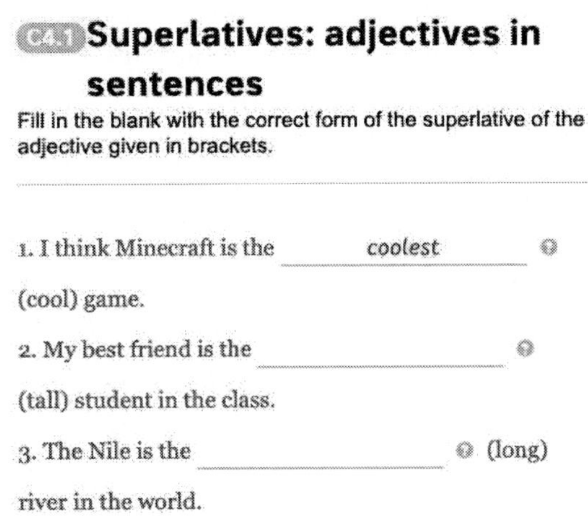

Figure 6: Activity C4.1 targeting superlatives

In this activity, students are given an adjective base form that has to be turned into its superlative form. According to specifications this is a fill-in-the-blanks activity, with items whose prompt consists of a sentence and whose answer length is a word. In addition, the activity is labeled with the language means in the curriculum *Superlative regular forms*, *Superlative irregular forms* and *Superlative most + Adj*, all of which are language means of level 2 in the hierarchy (see section 3.1).

Figure 7 shows a short answer activity. The activity includes a sentence as a prompt and requires complete sentence as a response. This activity gets the level 2 label *Sentences using the simple past*, a language structure appearing in the curriculum.

For this tutoring system, activity specification requires not only writing the instructions and

Figure 7: Activity T8.5 on past simple negation

prompts in them but also entering a list of correct answers. For the activity in Figure 6, the expected answers are the superlative forms of the corresponding adjectives, but for the activity in Figure 7 the expected answers are the negated version of the sentences, such as "Emma did not play tennis" or "You did not build a sand castle", for the first two items, respectively.

It is such activity specifications that are sent to the NLP-module performing the annotation of finer-grained language means (level 3).

4.2 Automatically generated properties

The first step of the automatic annotation process is the identification of language means based on the activity specification, using the NLP resources we introduced in section 3.

The second step performed in the annotation process distinguishes between so-called receptive and productive skills given that any linguistic phenomenon can be practiced in the context of understanding or producing language. What elements of an item are considered receptive or productive depends on the activity type. For fill-in-the-blanks activities, such as the one in Figure 6, the text in the expected answers for each blank constitutes the productive part (e.g, "coolest" in the first gap). In contrast, the language found in the text surrounding the blanks is handled as receptive since learners use them to complete the answer (e.g., "I think Minecraft is the ... (cool) game."). For short answer tasks, the receptive part are the prompts, and the productive parts are the answers to be elicited from the learners. For example, in Figure 9, the prompt "Emma played tennis" from the activity shown in Figure 7 is analyzed as language practiced in receptive mode (SyntAffirmativeSentenceSimplePast), while "Emma didn't play tennis." is language practiced in the productive mode (SyntNegativeSentenceSimplePast).

4.3 Information visualization

On this basis, we can systematically visualize the language means found in a given activity. Didi includes a visualization module that uses spider web charts to present this information.

Figure 8 illustrates the output for the fill-in-the-blanks activity targeting superlative forms we saw in Figure 6. We see that language means at the word and sentence level are classified as receptive or productive. For instance, a target goal at the word level, *SuperlativeFormRegularHigherDegree*, is classified as receptive once for "coolest", which is given as a sample answer, and as productive multiple times for gaps such as "tallest" and "longest", appearing in items 2 and 3 of the activity, respectively. At the sentence level, the target language means *AffirmativeSuperlativeSentence* and *InterrogativeSuperlativeSentence* are classified as productive, corresponding to the sentence containing the expected answer. Non-target means, such as *SyntAffirmativeSentencePresentSimple*, the rule for which was exemplified in Figure 4, are also represented in the spider web chart and can also be classified as receptive or productive.

Similarly, Figure 9 shows the spider web chart for the activity we saw in Figure 7, the one on the negative sentences in the past. In this activity, the affirmative sentences given as the prompts are classified as receptive, for instance, as *SyntAffirmativeSentenceSimplePast* at the sentence level. The expected answers contain the language mean *SyntNegativeSentenceSimplePast*, also at the sentence level and are classified as productive. In this activity, the annotation does not include non-target language means outside of the learning unit on tenses.

5 Applications of the approach

The approach described to enrich activity models is useful both from a pedagogical perspective for the design and selection of activities in relation to the curriculum and from the perspective of designing adaptive tutoring systems, where it supports the implementation of activity sequencing.

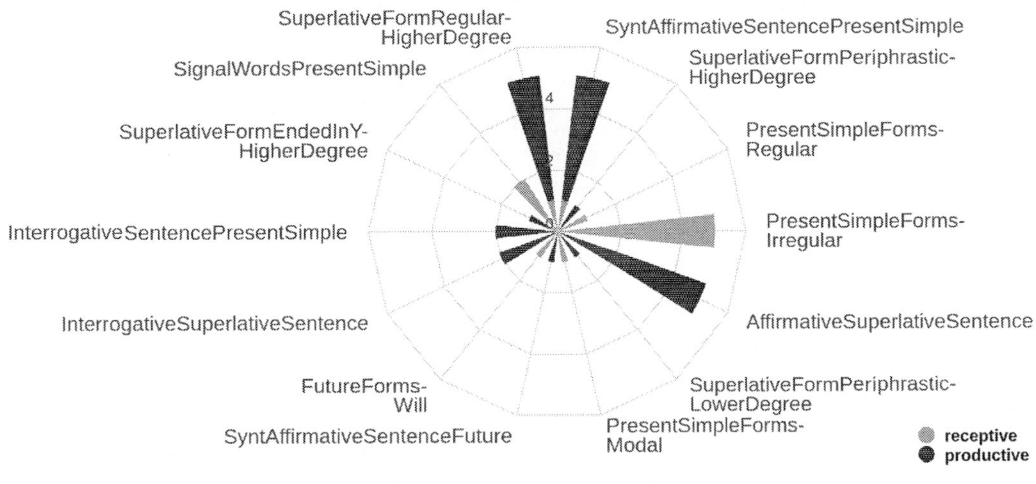

Figure 8: Visualization of annotated language means for activity C4.1

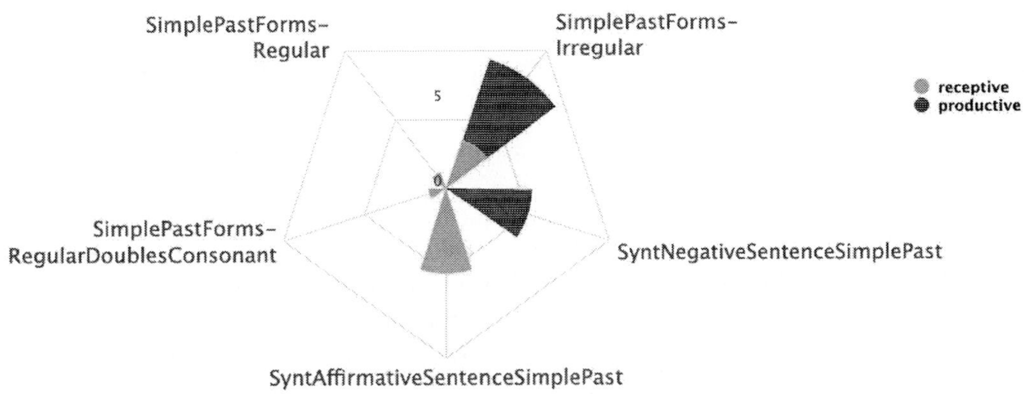

Figure 9: Visualization of annotated language means for activity T8.5

5.1 Evaluating curriculum coverage

A first approach to evaluating curriculum coverage can be carried out at the most abstract level of description, as in Table 2.

The table shows the number of automatically identified target and non-target language means at the receptive and productive level for the current set of activities implemented in four learning units. Pedagogically speaking, the table reflects that there are in total 845 opportunities either to produce (482) or to understand (363) one of the target language means of the tenses topic. We can also see that the numbers for the other three topics (comparatives, conditional sentences type 2 and elative clauses) are smaller. This tells us about the number of activities written for each of the topics which, as shown in the last column, is quite imbalanced – productive target language means in tenses amount to 56% of the opportunities to produce a piece of language in the current version of the materials.

The table also indicates that while tenses, comparatives and conditional sentences present a relatively balanced number of opportunities to practice target productive and receptive skills, relative clauses has a very low proportion (7%) of opportunities to practice target receptive skills. In this case a manual inspection of the activities in relative clauses confirms that the sequence of activities includes much more production activities than receptive ones.

If we take a look at the numbers under non-target language means, we see these are much higher and proportionally bigger for comparatives, conditional sentences type 2 and relative clauses. For instance, for comparatives the total number of non-target language means adds up to 417 (121

Table 2: Language means automatically identified in the activities of four learning units

	TARGET		NON-TARGET		
LEARNING UNIT	PROD.	REC.	PROD.	REC.	ACTIVITIES
tenses	482	363	133	152	49
comparatives	84	107	121	296	27
cond. sent. type 2	209	237	404	672	30
relative clauses	95	7	263	301	20
TOTAL	870	714	921	1,421	126

+ 296) while the total number of target language means adds up to 191 (84 + 107). A plausible explanation for this is the fact that although the learning of comparatives often focuses on word formation (building its forms) or some essential syntactic patterns (... ADJ *than* ..., ... *as* ADJ *as* ...), it is usually learned in the context of comparing different options (e.g., travel preferences, product prices and quality, etc.); since making comparisons requires the use of sentences that include different tenses and structures, a variety of non-target structures is expected here. Similar interpretations can be made for conditional sentences type 2 and relative clauses, two topics for which the use of sentences with all their underlying properties is required.

Finer-grained analyses of curriculum coverage are possible by quantifying the language means included in the materials as shown in Tables 3 and 4.

Table 3: Tenses: distribution of language means by level 1 categories

	TARGET		NON-TARGET	
CATEGORY	PROD.	REC.	PROD.	REC.
Word formation	248	233	95	106
Sentence structure	224	107	38	39
Language use	10	23	0	7
TOTAL	482	363	133	152

Table 3 offers a level 1 characterization of the opportunities to learn word formation, sentence structure and language use at the receptive and productive level on the unit on tenses. We can see that target language means are relatively proportionate between word formation and sentence structure, but not language use. At the same time, non-target means are much more frequent in word formation than in the other two categories.

Table 4 offers an even finer-grained representation of the distribution of language means – in this case for the category *word formation* in tenses. The table shows both target and non-target language means in productive and receptive skills. The horizontal line that divides the table in language means that are genuinely part of the grammar topic tenses and those that are not part of it.

Looking at the table, we can confirm that the unit on tenses has: (i) much more practice opportunities on the formation of irregular verbs (228 as target and 37 as non-target), than on any other verb form. However, we also see that some of the language means that are genuinely part of the grammar topic tenses are also used as non-target. This can be explained by activities in which a verb form is used to give a context in which then another verb form can be used. For instance, when practicing the past continuous forms, one will often see the pattern "*while* VP-PAST PARTICIPLE FORM ..., VP-PAST SIMPLE".

Now whether the presence and distribution of the language means as found in the learning activities in these units actually leads to mastery or not and whether they are compliant with a specific curricula is not within the scope of this paper. The goal of the paper is to show that this kind of evaluation is possible thanks to the information made explicit by the automated annotation strategy.

5.2 Automatic derivation of learner models

The rich activity models enable the ITS to generate learner models that track the progress of individual learners across activities. This serves two purposes: first, to inform learners about their observed competence in an inspectable, open learner model (Bull and Kay, 2006) and second, to inform the adaptive sequencing algorithm in Didi about the current level of proficiency of learners to suggest a suitable next exercise.

Whenever a learner works on an activity, the learner model for that learner records both the language means the learner was exposed to (i.e. the ones appearing in the activity) and the subset of language means that the learner was able to produce correctly. The learner model stores an update making explicit the exposure and accuracy for each level 3 language mean involved – together with a time stamp to enable temporal tracking. Taken together, the learner model records the dif-

Table 4: Detailed characterization of the language means found in *Tenses* at the morphology level

		TARGET		NON-TARGET	
LANGUAGE MEANS: LEVEL 2 & 3		PROD.	REC.	PROD.	REC.
FUTURE - *will*		4	1	0	1
PRES. CONT. FORMS		18	1	0	0
PRES. SIMPLE FORMS:	- IRREG	9	8	0	7
	- MODAL	5	10	0	2
	- REG	18	5	0	1
PAST CONT. FORMS		16	0	0	1
SIMPLE PAST FORMS:	- DOUBCONS	6	18	3	5
	- IN -Y	7	10	3	5
	- IN -E	17	24	5	12
	- IRREG	111	116	17	20
	- MODAL	2	5	0	1
	- REG	35	35	13	18
COMPARATIVE INTENS.:	- DOUBCONS	0	0	1	1
	- REG	0	0	0	2
COMPARATIVE EQUAL.		0	0	0	2
IMPERATIVE FORMS		0	0	0	9
PASSIVE - SIMPLE PAST		0	0	3	3
PAST PERFECT FORMS		0	0	19	6
PRES. PERFECT FORMS		0	0	30	3
REFLEXIVE PRONOUN		0	0	0	3
REL. PRON. - SUBJECT		0	0	1	4
TOTAL		248	233	95	106

ference between what language means an exercise exposed a learner to and which of them the learner was able to produce. The learner model is updated independent of whether the language means have been marked as target or non-target.

The open learner model in Didi presents the collected information structured in two levels (Figure 10). On the top, the system presents the collected evidence aggregated for language means at level 2, providing the learner with an overview on the performance for all the pedagogically relevant categories. If learners want to get more detailed insights, the system displays a more detailed view of language means of level 3 below the aggregate view (bottom graph). For each of the level 2 labels, this detailed view lists a learner's performance for each of the language means of level 3 belonging to this level 2 label according to the domain model (cf. Figure 3), distinguishing receptive from productive skills. The learner model also presents language structures in the dimension *interactive* – learning opportunities in which language means need to be selected as opposed to typed in, e.g., in a multiple-choice task.

For example, in Figure 10, the category *VerbFormsSimplePast* appears in the top chart in the south east with a long green (correct usage) and shorter red (incorrect usage) bar. The bottom chart lists all the associated child language means, e.g., *SimplePastFormsRegular* or *SimplePastFormsModal*. This allows the learner to see which specific language means (s)he is struggling with the most – in this example it is *SimplePastFormsIrregular*.

5.3 Combining activity and learner models for adaptive sequencing

The learner and activity model together are the basis for the adaptive sequencing algorithm. This algorithm operates at the level of subsections within learning units, for which target structures are specified, and suggests a next suitable exercise to individual learners. In the first step, the system identifies the target language means that still need to be learned by filtering out all those structures for which the learner has obtained *mastery*. Mastery is assessed by comparing both the exposure to and accuracy achieved in the language means by externally defined thresholds in a configurable lookback window. Exposure is measured as the number of times an exercise provided an opportunity to practice a specific construction, and accuracy indicates how many times a specific learner was able to produce it correctly. The lookback window makes it possible to base decisions only on the recent performance, so that trying out different forms in earlier acquisition stages is not penalized. In the second step, the system queries exercises that contain the language means to be practiced by the learner. At this stage, Didi ranks the queried exercises using a linguistic affinity score by computing the closeness between the language

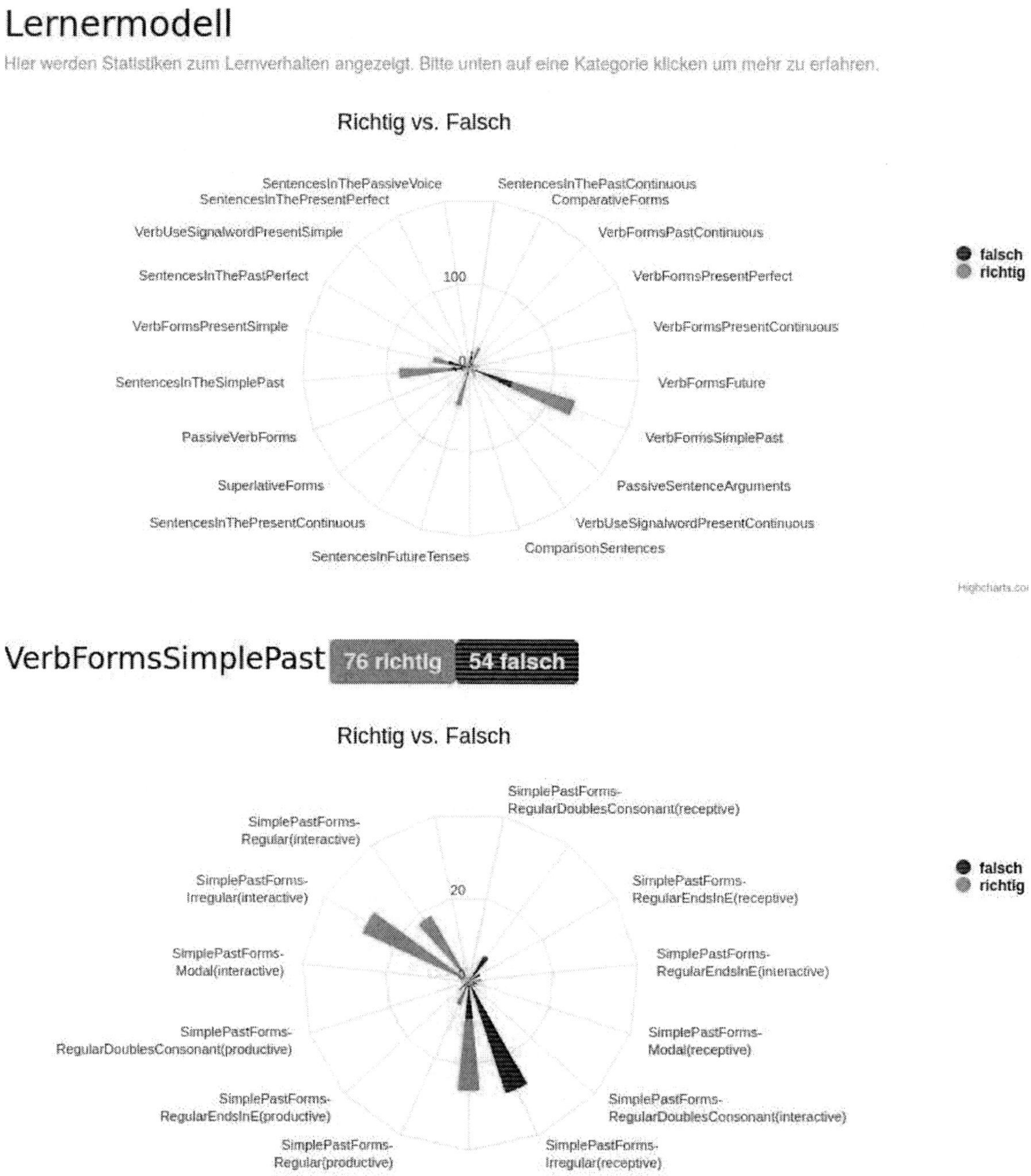

Figure 10: Open learner model visualizing performance on language means at level 2 (top) and level 3 (bottom)

means an activity offers and the current learning goals. The third step is to rank candidate exercises using pedagogically driven categories stored in the activity model (cf. Figure 5). For example, the adaptivity algorithm suggests closed activity types before open activities, activities with shorter gaps before activities with longer gaps, or activities where inflected forms are provided before tasks without any given lexical material. The automatically derived activity models allow for an activity selection process that not only takes into account what was actually learned as a target, but also everything learned as non-target.

6 Concluding remarks and future work

The work presented here shows how combining manual and automatic annotation of learning activities facilitates the enrichment of activity models. Making the linguistic properties explicit in this way supports a link between the language to be learned (expert model), the strategies to present this language as a learning goal (instruction model), and the language competence as recorded (learner model). The linguistically enriched activity models do not only take into account the language produced (or seen) when this was a learning goal, but also the language produced (or seen) as co-material – as a consequence of embedding the actual learning goals in more complex linguistic structures or larger language units.

While the approach described in this paper is fully implemented, it represents ongoing work and comes with certain limitations. First of all, there is currently no gold standard against which the accuracy of the NLP annotation module can be evaluated. However, the quantification of language means identified in the four learning units seems to indicate good face validity.

An additional limitation of the approach is that it only annotates language phenomena that appear in the input materials, which are used as a basis for specification. Comparing our aggregated annotations with resources such as the EGP informs us about the areas of language for which no activities exist – or appear only as non-target, which we have not systematically addressed yet.

Finally, the adaptivity algorithm described here is still under development and has not been tested in practice yet. Piloting and evaluating it in an authentic school context to assess the external validity is planned for the next project phase. We will conduct a randomized controlled field trial study for testing the effectiveness of adaptive sequencing of activities compared to static sequences defined in advance by teachers. Students across a range of different types of secondary schools will randomly be assigned to either the intervention group (adaptive sequences) or control group (static sequences). By employing a pre-post test design, we will be able to associate learning gains with experimental conditions and to test for which types of schools and learning goals adaptivity makes a difference.

Our most immediate goal at this point is to further develop both the knowledge hierarchy and the annotation rules. The sequencing algorithm requires a rich linguistic characterization and explicit interrelationships between specific language means. For instance, conditional type 2 sentences cannot be practiced if past simple forms and conditional forms have not been learned. Additionally, information from the expert model determining priorities between specific linguistic structures at a given point in the instruction plan can be used if more than one linguistic structure competes to be the "next" one.

In the mid-term, the creation of a gold-standard to evaluate the quality of the annotation process is also a task that we cannot escape. Since we have access to activities from other e-learning platforms, we can use those to perform a semi-automatic evaluation of the module. An evaluation from the perspective of the end-user in terms of the system's efficacy will be possible as soon as the system starts to be piloted in schools. For that purpose we will simulate learning paths that will then end up proposing "next tasks" that a teacher will then judge as pedagogically meaningful or not.

Acknowledgments

This research has been largely funded by the Robert-Bosch-Stiftung GmbH as part of the program "Förderung von Wissenschaft-Praxis-Kooperationen für Unterrichtskonzepte mit digitalen Medien".

References

Luiz Amaral. 2007. *Designing Intelligent Language Tutoring Systems: integrating Natural Language Processing technology into foreign language teaching*. Ph.D. thesis, The Ohio State University.

Luiz Amaral and Detmar Meurers. 2011. On using intelligent computer-assisted language learning in real-life foreign language teaching and learning. *ReCALL*, 23(1):4–24.

Lyle F. Bachman and Adrian S. Palmer. 1996. *Language Testing in Practice: Designing and Developing Useful Language Tests.* Oxford University Press.

H. Douglas Brown. 2007. *Principles Of Language Learning and Teaching*, 5th edition. Pearson Education.

Susan Bull and Judy Kay. 2006. *Student models that invite the learner in: The SMILI open learner modelling framework.* Citeseer.

Maria Chinkina and Detmar Meurers. 2016. Linguistically-aware information retrieval: Providing input enrichment for second language learners. In *Proceedings of the 11th Workshop on Innovative Use of NLP for Building Educational Applications (BEA)*, pages 188–198, San Diego, CA. ACL.

Inn-Chull Choi. 2016. Efficacy of an ICALL tutoring system and process-oriented corrective feedback. *Computer Assisted Language Learning*, 29(2):334–364.

Jinho D Choi and Martha Palmer. 2012. Fast and robust part-of-speech tagging using dynamic model selection. In *Proceedings of the 50th Annual Meeting of the ACL*, pages 363–367.

Council of Europe. 2020. *Common European Framework of Reference for Languages: Learning, teaching, assessment – Companion Volume.* Cambridge University Press, Cambridge.

Zoltán Dörnyei and Peter Skehan. 2003. *Individual Differences in Second Language Learning*, chapter 18. John Wiley & Sons, Ltd.

Sheila Estaire and Javier Zanón. 1994. *Planning classwork: A task-based approach.* Educational Language Teaching. MacMillan-Heinemann, Oxford.

David Ferrucci and Adam Lally. 2004. UIMA: An architectural approach to unstructured information processing in the corporate research environment. *Natural Language Engineering*, 10(3–4):327–348.

S.M. Gass and A. Mackey. 2013. *The Routledge Handbook of Second Language Acquisition.* Routledge Handbooks in Applied Linguistics. Taylor & Francis.

Susan M. Gass and Alison Mackey. 2015. Input, interaction and output in second language acquisition. In Bill VanPatten and Jessica Williams, editors, *Theories in Second Language Acquisition: An Introduction (2nd edition).* Routledge, New York and London.

Trude Heift. 2010. Prompting in CALL: A longitudinal study of learner uptake. *Modern Language Journal*, 94(2):198–216.

Peter Kluegl, Martin Toepfer, Philip-Daniel Beck, Georg Fette, and Frank Puppe. 2016. Uima ruta: Rapid development of rule-based information extraction applications. *Natural Language Engineering*, 22(1):1–40.

Kultusministerium. 2016. Englisch als erste Fremdsprache [English as a first foreign language]. Bildungsplan des Gymnasiums 2016 [State curriculum for academic track schools 2016]. Ministerium für Kultus, Jugend und Sport, Baden Württemberg.

Shawn Loewen and Masatoshi Sato. 2017. *The Routledge handbook of instructed second language acquisition.* Routledge New York.

Wenting Ma, Olusola O. Adesope, John C. Nesbit, and Qing Liu. 2014. Intelligent tutoring systemsand learning outcomes: A meta-analysis. *Journal of Educational Psychology*, 106(4):901–918.

Melinda Martin-Beltrán, Natalia L. Guzman, and Pei-Jie Jenny Chen. 2017. 'let's think about it together:' how teachers differentiate discourse to mediate collaboration among linguistically diverse students. *Language Awareness*, 26(1):41–58.

Detmar Meurers, Kordula De Kuthy, Florian Nuxoll, Björn Rudzewitz, and Ramon Ziai. 2019. Scaling up intervention studies to investigate real-life foreign language learning in school. *Annual Review of Applied Linguistics*, 39:161–188.

Detmar Meurers, Kordula De Kuthy, Verena Möller, Florian Nuxoll, Björn Rudzewitz, and Ramon Ziai. 2018. Digitale Differenzierung benötigt Informationen zu Sprache, Aufgabe und Lerner. Zur Generierung von individuellem Feedback in einem interaktiven Arbeitsheft. *FLuL – Fremdsprachen Lehren und Lernen*, 47(2):64–82.

Detmar Meurers, Ramon Ziai, Luiz Amaral, Adriane Boyd, Aleksandar Dimitrov, Vanessa Metcalf, and Niels Ott. 2010. Enhancing authentic web pages for language learners. In *Proceedings of the 5th Workshop on Innovative Use of NLP for Building Educational Applications (BEA)*, pages 10–18, Los Angeles. ACL.

Guido Minnen, John Carroll, and Darren Pearce. 2001. Applied morphological processing of English. *Natural Language Engineering*, 7(3):207–233.

Noriko Nagata. 2009. Robo-Sensei's NLP-based error detection and feedback generation. *CALICO Journal*, 26(3):562–579.

Björn Rudzewitz, Ramon Ziai, Kordula De Kuthy, and Detmar Meurers. 2017. Developing a web-based workbook for English supporting the interaction of students and teachers. In *Proceedings of the Joint*

6th Workshop on NLP for Computer Assisted Language Learning and 2nd Workshop on NLP for Research on Language Acquisition, pages 36–46.

Björn Rudzewitz, Ramon Ziai, Kordula De Kuthy, Verena Möller, Florian Nuxoll, and Detmar Meurers. 2018. Generating feedback for English foreign language exercises. In *Proceedings of the 13th Workshop on Innovative Use of NLP for Building Educational Applications (BEA)*, pages 127–136. ACL.

Helmut Schmid. 2005. A programming language for finite state transducers. In *Proceedings of the 5th International Workshop on Finite State Methods in Natural Language Processing*, pages 308–309.

Carol Ann Tomlinson. 2015. Teaching for excellence in academically diverse classrooms. *Society*, 52(3):203–209.

Kurt VanLehn. 2011. The relative effectiveness of human tutoring, intelligent tutoring systems, and other tutoring systems. *Educational Psychologist*, 46(4):197–221.

Ramon Ziai, Florian Nuxoll, Kordula De Kuthy, Björn Rudzewitz, and Detmar Meurers. 2019. The impact of spelling correction and task context on short answer assessment for intelligent tutoring systems. In *Proceedings of the 8th Workshop on NLP for Computer Assisted Language Learning*, pages 93–99, Turku, Finland. ACL.

Ramon Ziai, Björn Rudzewitz, Kordula De Kuthy, Florian Nuxoll, and Detmar Meurers. 2018. Feedback strategies for form and meaning in a real-life language tutoring system. In *Proceedings of the 7th Workshop on Natural Language Processing for Computer-Assisted Language Learning (NLP4CALL)*, pages 91–98. ACL.

DaLAJ - a dataset for linguistic acceptability judgments for Swedish

Elena Volodina[1], Yousuf Ali Mohammed[1], Julia Klezl[2]
University of Gothenburg, Sweden
[1]name.surname1.surname2@svenska.gu.se
[2]gusklezju@student.gu.se

Abstract

We present DaLAJ 1.0, a **Da**taset for **L**inguistic **A**cceptability **J**udgments for Swedish, comprising 9 596 sentences in its first version. DaLAJ is based on the SweLL second language learner data (Volodina et al., 2019), consisting of essays at different levels of proficiency. To make sure the dataset can be freely available despite the GDPR regulations, we have sentence-scrambled learner essays and removed part of the metadata about learners, keeping for each sentence only information about the mother tongue and the level of the course where the essay has been written. We use the normalized version of learner language as the basis for DaLAJ sentences, and keep only one error per sentence. We repeat the same sentence for each individual correction tag used in the sentence. For DaLAJ 1.0 four error categories of 35 available in SweLL are used, all connected to lexical or word-building choices. The dataset is included in the SwedishGlue benchmark.[1] Below, we describe the format of the dataset, our insights and motivation for the chosen approach to data sharing.

1 Introduction

Grammatical and linguistic acceptability is an extensive area of research that has been studied for generations by theoretical linguists (e.g. Chomsky, 1957), and lately by cognitive and computational linguists (e.g. Keller, 2000; Lau et al., 2020; Warstadt et al., 2019). Acceptability of sentences is defined as "the extent to which a sentence is permissible or acceptable to native speakers of the language." (Lau et al., 2015, p.1618), and there have been different approaches to studying it. Most work views acceptability as a binary phenomenon: the sentence is either acceptable/ grammatical or not (e.g. Warstadt et al., 2019). Lau et al. (2014) show that the phenomenon is in fact gradient and is dependent on a larger context than just one sentence. While most experiments are theoretically-driven, the practical value of this research has been also underlined, especially with respect to language learning and error detection (Wagner et al., 2009; Heilman et al., 2014; Daudaravicius et al., 2016).

Datasets for acceptability judgments require linguistic samples that are unacceptable, which requires a source of so-called negative examples. Previously, such samples have been either manually constructed, artificially generated through machine translation (Lau et al., 2020), prepared by automatically distorting acceptable samples e.g. by deleting or inserting words or inflections (Wagner et al., 2009) or collected from theoretical linguistics books (Warstadt et al., 2019). Using samples produced by language learners has not been mentioned in connection to acceptability and grammaticality studies. However, there are obvious benefits of getting authentic errors that automatic systems may meet in real-life. Another benefit of reusing samples from learner corpora is that they often contain not only corrections, but also labels describing the corrections. The major benefit, though, is that (un)acceptability judgments come from experts, i.e. teachers, assessors or trained assistants, and are therefore reliable.

[1] SwedishGlue (Swe. SuperLim) is a collection of datasets for training and/or evaluating language models for a range of Natural Language Understanding (NLU) tasks.

Elena Volodina, Yousuf Ali Mohammed and Julia Klezl 2021. DaLAJ – a dataset for linguistic acceptability judgments for Swedish. *Proceedings of the 10th Workshop on Natural Language Processing for Computer Assisted Language Learning (NLP4CALL 2021)*. Linköping Electronic Conference Proceedings 177: 28–37.

Categories	Explanation	A-lev	B-lev	C-lev	Total
O-Comp	Problem with compounding	252	62	232	546
L-Der	Word formation problem (derivation or compounding)	193	124	404	721
L-FL	Non-Swedish word corrected to Swedish word	46	17	26	89
L-W	Wrong word or phrase	1157	562	1723	3442
Total		**1648**	**765**	**2385**	**4798**

Table 1: Dataset overview, with number of sentences per correction tag, level and in total

Approximate level	Nr essays	Nr labels
A:Beginner	289	11 180
B:Intermediate	45	5 119
C:Advanced	168	12 986
Total	**502**	**29 285**

Table 2: Statistics over the SweLL data

2 Dataset description

We use the error-annotated learner corpus SweLL (Volodina et al., 2019) as a source of "unacceptable" sentences and select sentences containing corrections of the type that is of relevance to the SwedishGlue benchmark[2] (Adesam et al., 2020).

In the current version, four *lexical error types* are included into the DaLAJ dataset (see Section 2.2). The resulting dataset contains 4 798 sentence pairs (correct-incorrect), where the two sentences in each sentence pair are identical to each other except for one error. In total, DaLAJ 1.0 contains 9 596 sentences (which is a sum of unacceptable sentences and their corrected "twin" sentences). To compare, Lau et al. (2014) use a dataset of 2 500 sentences and Warstadt et al. (2019) have about 10 700 sentences for a similar task. We have a possibility to extend the DaLAJ dataset by other correction types (spelling, morphological or syntactical) in future versions. The full SweLL dataset contains 29 285 correction tags, of which 25 878 may become relevant for the current task (omitting punctuation, consequence and unintelligibility correction tags).

2.1 The source corpus

The SweLL data (Volodina et al., 2019) has been collected over four years (2017-2020) from adult learners of Swedish from formal educational settings, such as courses and tests. The collection contains about 680 pseudonymized essays in total, with 502 of those manually normalized (i.e. rewritten to standard Swedish) and annotated for the nature of the correction (aka error annotation). Table 2 shows the statistics over SweLL in number of essays and correction tags per level. Levels of the sentences correspond to the level of the course that learners were taking when they wrote essays. The essays represent several levels, namely:

`A` - beginner level
`B` - intermediate level
`C` - advanced level

The data is saved in two versions: the original and the normalized, with correction labels assigned to the links between the two versions. The 502 corr-annotated essays contain 29 285 corrections distributed over 35 correction tags, as listed in Appendix A.

2.2 Selection of (un)grammatical sentences

The linguistic acceptability task in the SwedishGlue is described as a natural language understanding (NLU) task conceptualized as binary judgments from a perspective relevant for research on language learning, language planning etc. (Adesam et al., 2020). Semantic aspects of the sentence are the main focus of this task. This deviates from the type of language included into the CoLA dataset available through GLUE (Warstadt et al., 2019), where also morphological and syntactic violations are included. In DaLAJ 1.0, we have selected four correction types from the SweLL corpus that would maximally correspond to the need of semantic interpretation of the context, namely `L-W`, `L-Der`, `L-FL`, `O-Comp` (Rudebeck and Sundberg, 2020), described below.

L-W: Wrong word or phrase. The `L-W` tag represents the correction category *wrong word or phrase*. It is used when a word or phrase in the original text has been replaced by another word or

[2]SwedishGlue is a collection of datasets for training and/or evaluating language models for a range of Natural Language Understanding (NLU) tasks.

original sentence	corrected sentence	error indices (original)	corrected indices	error-corr pair	error label	L1	Approximate level
Förr i tiden kunde vi byta en sak till en annan .	Förr i tiden kunde vi byta en sak mot en annan .	34-37	34-36	till--mot	L-W	Polska	B:Fortsättning
Jag kan ta några exempel av betydelsen av pengar .	Jag kan ta några exempel på betydelsen av pengar .	25-26	25-26	av--på	L-W	Somaliska	B:Fortsättning
Och där efter köper vi nästan allt vi behöver .	Och därefter köper vi nästan allt vi behöver .	4-12	4-11	där efter--därefter	O-Comp	Somaliska	B:Fortsättning
För det andra är det nyckeln av livet .	För det andra är det nyckeln till livet .	29-30	29-32	av--till	L-W	Somaliska	B:Fortsättning
Det är svårt ibland men det kommer inte på engång .	Det är svårt ibland men det kommer inte på en gång .	43-48	43-49	engång--en gång	O-Comp	Somaliska	B:Fortsättning
Bostäder i D-hemland är ett lite hett topik att diskutera .	Bostäder i D-hemland är ett lite hett ämne att diskutera .	38-42	38-41	topik--ämne	L-FL	Ungerska	A:Nybörjare
Bostäder i D-hemland är ett lite hett ämne att diskussera .	Bostäder i D-hemland är ett lite hett ämne att diskutera .	47-56	47-55	diskussera--diskutera	L-FL	Ungerska	A:Nybörjare
Många lägenheter och hus är gamla och har dålig energi-niveå .	Många lägenheter och hus är gamla och har dålig energinivå .	48-59	48-57	energi-niveå--energinivå	O-Comp	Ungerska	A:Nybörjare
Man betalar mycket i vintern , vilket är likadant som i Sverige .	Man betalar mycket på vintern , vilket är likadant som i Sverige .	19-19	19-20	i--på	L-W	Ungerska	A:Nybörjare
Man betalar mycket på vintern , vilket är det samma som i Sverige .	Man betalar mycket på vintern , vilket är likadant som i Sverige .	42-50	42-49	det samma--likadant	L-W	Ungerska	A:Nybörjare

Figure 1: An excerpt from the dataset

phrase in the normalized version. It is placed on units which are exchanged rather than corrected. For example,

`Alla blir *busiga med sociala medier →`

`Alla blir upptagna med sociala medier`

which may be verbatim translated as

`Everyone is *naughty with social media →`

`Everyone is busy with social media`

Note the Engligh influence on the use of the word `*busiga` to convey the meaning that someone is `*busy` (Swe `upptagen`), the Swedish word `busig` meaning `mischievous, naughty`.

L-Der: Word formation. The `L-Der` tag represents the correction category *deviant word formation*. It is used for corrections of the internal morphological structure of word stems, both with regard to compounding and to derivation.

The `L-Der` tag is exclusively used for links between one-word units (not necessarily one-token units, since a word may mistakenly be written as two tokens), where the normalized word has kept at least one root morpheme from the original word, but where another morpheme has been removed, added, exchanged or had its form altered. For example,

`De är *stressiga på grund av studier →`

`De är stressade på grund av studier`

which may be translated as

`They are *stressy because of the studies →`

`They are stressed because of the studies`

Note that `*stressiga` uses an existing derivation affix `-ig(a)`, which is wrong in this context, instead of the correct suffix `-ade, stressade`.

L-FL: Foreign word corrected to Swedish. The `L-FL` tag is used for *words from a foreign (non-Swedish) language* which have been corrected to a Swedish word. It may also be applied to words which have certain non-Swedish traits due to influence from a foreign language. For example,

`Jag och min *family →`

`Jag och min familj`

`English: I and my family`

O-Comp: Spaces and hyphens between words. The `O-Comp` tag is used for corrections which involve the removal of a space between two words which have been interpreted as making up a compound in the normalized text version, or, more rarely, the adding of a space between two words.

It may also be used for corrections regarding the use of hyphens in *compounds*. Some examples,

`Jag kände mig *jätte *konstig →`

`Jag kände mig jättekonstig`

`English: I felt very strange`

Distribution of the correction tags in the DaLAJ 1.0 dataset is shown in Table 1.

2.3 Data format

The task of linguistic acceptability judgments is traditionally performed on the *sentence level*, where each sentence includes *maximum one deviation*. In real life learner-written sentences may contain several errors, but it has been shown that training algorithms on samples with focus on one error only produces better results than when mixing several errors in one sentence; extending the context to a paragraph may further improve the results (Katinskaia and Yangarber, 2021). Paragraphs in learner data, however, are not predictable or well defined, and on several occasions in the SweLL data entire essays consist of one paragraph only. Including in the DaLAJ dataset full paragraphs, in certain cases equivalent to full essays, entails risks of revealing author identities through indications of author-related events or other identifiers despite our meticulous work on pseudonymization of essays (Volodina et al., 2020; Megyesi et al., 2018). We assess, therefore, that we have no possibility to include paragraphs into the dataset due to the restrictions imposed by the GDPR, so we follow the generally accepted standard of single sentences with single deviations.

For each correction label used in the corpus data, we take the corrected target sentence and preserve only one erroneous segment in it to make it "unacceptable". This means that the same sentence can be repeated several times in the dataset, with different segments/deviations being in the focus. Positive samples are represented by the corrected sentences. We have data in a tab separated file format, with eight columns, namely:

1. Original (i.e. unacceptable) sentence, e.g. `Men pengarna är inte *alls` (Eng. But money is not *at all)
2. Corrected sentence, e.g. `Men pengarna är inte allt` (Eng. But money is not everything)
3. Error string indices, e.g. `21-24`
4. Correct string indices, e.g. `21-24`
5. Error-correction pair, e.g. `alls-allt`
6. Error label, e.g. `L-W`
7. Mother tongue(s) (L1), e.g. `Somali`
8. Approximate level, e.g. `B:Intermediate`

Figure 1 shows an excerpt from the dataset. Note that some of the sentences in the "Corrected sentence" column are repeated more than once. The corresponding original sentences contain a new error focus each time. The dataset is (by default) balanced with respect to the number of correct and incorrect samples, however, correct samples contain a number of duplicates which should be complimented by a corresponding number of unique correct sentences, which is something we will add in the next release of the dataset. The dataset is not equally balanced as far as number of sentences per level or per correction code are concerned, which is a more challenging problem.

CoLA dataset authors have explicitly tested that the vocabulary used in their dataset belongs to the 100 000 most frequent words in the language (Warstadt et al., 2019). In the case of DaLAJ, we have not done any such investigation since we believe that the vocabulary used by second language learners cannot be so advanced as to be outside the 100K most frequent words.

Initial experiments on the dataset, data splits and first baselines are reported in an extended version of this article, available at arXiv.org. The DaLAJ 1.0 dataset is freely available at the SwedishGlue webpage.[3]

3 First analysis

We see multiple advantages to use the proposed format for L2 data. Apart from a potential to share the data with wider community of researchers, it also (1) helps expand the data (each original sentence potentially generating several sentences) and (2) helps focus on one error only, facilitating fine-grained analysis of model performance as well as human evaluation of model predictions.

Our analysis has suggested, that the DaLAJ 1.0 dataset needs to be cleaned in several ways. First, the SweLL corpus contains a number of essays where learners add reference lists by the end of essays. Naturally, punctuation in reference lists is non-standard, among others not always containing full stop which sabbotages sentence segmentation. Besides, references are syntactically elliptical and do not fit into the standard language. We would

[3]https://spraakbanken.gu.se/en/resources/swedishglue

need to clean the dataset of all such sentences to ensure more objective training and testing.

Second, some sentences contain "hanging" titles or e-mail headers. Those hanging elements have not been separated by a full stop in the original essays, and have been prefixed to the next following sentence, which, again, can interfere with model training, e.g. `(Swe) En B-institution-entusiast Hej Segerstad kommun !` > `(Eng) A B-institute-enthusiast Hi Segerstad municipality !`

Yet another observed weakness of the DaLAJ 1.0 dataset, is that the positive sentences are repetitive. Since the models need to be trained on unique samples, we plan to exchange the non-unique ones with other sentences. Luckily, positive samples are easier to find than negative ones. We plan to use a corpus of L2 coursebooks graded for levels of proficiency, COCTAILL (Volodina et al., 2014), to replace duplicate sentences with the ones of equivalent level, and as far as possible, having similar linguistic features and length. Another potential source of in-domain positive sentences are SweLL sentences that do not contain any correction tags. However, such sentences are not many, and we would still need to use COCTAILL sentences or some other correct sentences.

The described changes will be introduced in DaLAJ 1.1 and in the test test for DaLAJ 1.0.

Finally, there is an important difference between the type of sentences used in CoLA and DaLAJ datasets. CoLA sentences are constructed manually for linguistic course books exemplifying various theoretically important linguistic features, and do not require wider context to interpret; whereas DaLAJ sentences are torn out of their natural context, and contain anaphoric references and elliptical structures. However, the applied value of training (machine learning) algorithms on DaLAJ sentences is higher than CoLA sentences (as we imagine that) since such models can be used in language learning context for writing support.

4 Reflections on access to learner data

Datasets and corpora collected from (second) language learners contain private information represented both on the metadata level and - depending on the topic - in the texts. Presence of personal information makes those datasets non-trivial to share with the public in a FAIR[4] way (Frey et al., 2020; Volodina et al., 2020), to say nothing of a potential to use such data for *shared tasks*. This is rather unfortunate since collection and preparation of such corpora is an extremely time-consuming and expensive process. Language learner datasets can seldom boast big sizes appropriate for training data-greedy machine learning algorithms, and could therefore benefit from aggregating data from several sources - provided they are accessible. Access to such data, besides, ensures transparency of the research and stimulates its fast development (MacWhinney, 2017; Marsden et al., 2018).

As data owners, we have to face two contradictory forces: one requiring open sharing, and the other preventing it. Among advocates for sharing data openly we see

- national and international funding agencies, e.g. Swedish Research Council[5] or European Commission[6], requiring guarantees from grant holders that any produced data will be made available for other researchers,
- national and international infrastructures, e.g. Clarin[7] or SLABank,[8] and
- updated journal policies (e.g. The Modern Language Journal).[9]

On the more restrictive side, we have national Ethical Review Authorities[10] and the General Data Protection Regulation, GDPR (Commission, 2016), described shortly below.

The Swedish Ethical Review Authority currently requires that we keep the original data (e.g. hand-written/ non-transcribed/ non-pseudonymized essays) for ten years after the project end so that researchers, who may question the trustworthiness of the original data handling, can require access to the original data for inspection. This means that the data owners need to keep mappings between learner names and their corpus IDs to make it possible to link de-identified and pseudonymized essays to their original versions.

General Data Protection Regulation sets certain

[4]FAIR: Findable, Accessible, Interoperable, Reusable (Wilkinson et al., 2016)

[5]https://www.vr.se/english/mandates/open-science/open-access-to-research-data.html

[6]https://ec.europa.eu/info/research-and-innovation/strategy/goals-research-and-innovation-policy/open-science/open-access_en

[7]https://www.clarin.eu/

[8]https://slabank.talkbank.org/

[9]https://onlinelibrary.wiley.com/journal/15404781

[10]https://www.government.se/government-agencies/the-swedish-ethics-review-authority-etikprovningsmyndigheten/

limitations on the data where personal data occurs, among others:

• learner identities should be protected, e.g. pseudonymized or de-identified;

• data need to be removed if any of the data providers (=learners) requests that;

• users that are granted access to the data should have affiliation inside Europe; and

• questions that users can work with are limited to the ones stated in the consent forms, in the case of SweLL encompassing research on and didactic applications for language learning.

To meet these requirements, data owners need to administer data access through an application form, where applicants have to be asked about their geographical location and research questions, and need to be informed about the limitations of spreading data to unauthorized users, etc. Users outside Europe can file an application to the university lawyers who have to consider them on a case-to-case basis. The GDPR applies to the data as long as a mapping of learner names with their corpus IDs (as required by the Ethical Review Authorities) is not destroyed. At a certain point of time (currently 10 years) the mapping key will be destroyed and the data will no longer be under the GDPR protection.

In both cases, a 10-year quarantine is obligatory. The restrictions above do not seem to hamper most of the potential EU-based researchers from getting access to the data in its entirety, especially researchers working with qualitative analysis of the data inside a limited project group, e.g. Second Language Acquisition researchers or researchers on language assessment. However, when it comes to the NLP field, the most effective way to stimulate research is to organize *shared tasks* or provide access to testing and evaluation datasets without any extra administration, as it is, for example, done in the GLUE[11] and SuperGLUE[12] benchmarks (Wang et al., 2018, 2019).

From the above it follows that data owners need to keep a promise to the funding agencies to make the data open, and at the same time, to follow the legislation and keep the data locked within Europe and only for research questions dealing with language learning. Being representatives of a "trapped researcher" group, we have been considering how to make learner data available for a wider audience. For a range of NLP tasks we suggest, thus, sharing L2 data in a sentence scrambled way with limited amount of socio-demographic metadata, for example for error detection & correction tasks. The DaLAJ dataset is a proof-of-concept attempt in this direction.

Ultimately, the education NLP community working with L2 datasets would win by setting up a benchmark with available (multilingual) datasets in the same way as GLUE benchmark is doing for Natural Language Understanding (NLU) tasks.

[11]https://gluebenchmark.com/

[12]https://super.gluebenchmark.com/

5 Concluding remarks

We have presented a new dataset for Swedish which can be used for a variety of tasks in Natural Language Processing (NLP) or Second Language Acquisition (SLA) contexts. We see our contributions both with regards to the dataset, as well as with suggesting a format for L2 datasets that may allow sharing learner data more openly in the GDPR age.

In the near future, we will test binary linguistic acceptability classification on the current selection of correction categories, and on the full SweLL dataset (all correction tags), per error category and level, establishing baselines for this task on this dataset. We plan to correlate the classification results with correction categories, levels and L1s. Further, we plan to apply models, trained on DaLAJ, to real learner data containing multiple errors per sentence, to assess the effect of data manipulation (i.e. original essays > DaLAJ format) on algorithm training. Proofreading the dataset and addressing identified weaknesses and errors is another direction for the future work.

In some more distant future we would like to organize shared tasks using DaLAJ. Apart from binary classification for linguistic acceptability judgments, we see a potential of using DaLAJ dataset (in extended version to cover the full correction tagset) for a range of other tasks, including:

• error detection (identification of error location)

• error classification (labeling for error type)

• error correction (generating correction suggestions)

• first language identification (given samples written by learners, to identify their mother tongues)

• classification of sentences by the level of proficiency of its writers, and other potential tasks.

Acknowledgments

This work has been supported by *Nationella Språkbanken* – jointly funded by its 10 partner institutions and the Swedish Research Council (dnr 2017-00626), as well as partly supported by a grant from the Swedish Riksbankens Jubileumsfond (SweLL - research infrastructure for Swedish as a second language, dnr IN16-0464:1).

References

Yvonne Adesam, Aleksandrs Berdicevskis, and Felix Morger. 2020. SwedishGLUE–Towards a Swedish Test Set for Evaluating Natural Language Understanding Models. *Research Reports from the Department of Swedish. GU-ISS-2020-04.*

Noam Chomsky. 1957. *Syntactic structures*. The Hague: Mouton.

European Commission. 2016. *General data protection regulation.* Official Journal of the European Union, 59, 1-88.

Vidas Daudaravicius, Rafael E Banchs, Elena Volodina, and Courtney Napoles. 2016. A report on the automatic evaluation of scientific writing shared task. In *Proceedings of the 11th Workshop on Innovative Use of NLP for Building Educational Applications*, pages 53–62.

Jennifer-Carmen Frey, Alexander König, and Darja Fišer. 2020. Creating a learner corpus infrastructure: Experiences from making learner corpora available. In *ITM Web of Conferences*, volume 33, page 03006. EDP Sciences.

Michael Heilman, Aoife Cahill, Nitin Madnani, Melissa Lopez, Matthew Mulholland, and Joel Tetreault. 2014. Predicting grammaticality on an ordinal scale. In *Proceedings of the 52nd Annual Meeting of the Association for Computational Linguistics (Volume 2: Short Papers)*, pages 174–180.

Anisia Katinskaia and Roman Yangarber. 2021. Assessing Grammatical Correctness in Language Learning. In *Proceedings of the Sixteenth Workshop on Innovative Use of NLP for Building Educational Applications.*

Frank Keller. 2000. *Gradience in grammar: Experimental and computational aspects of degrees of grammaticality.* Ph.D. thesis.

Jey Han Lau, Carlos Armendariz, Shalom Lappin, Matthew Purver, and Chang Shu. 2020. How Furiously Can Colorless Green Ideas Sleep? Sentence Acceptability in Context. *Transactions of the Association for Computational Linguistics*, 8:296–310.

Jey Han Lau, Alexander Clark, and Shalom Lappin. 2014. Measuring gradience in speakers' grammaticality judgements. In *Proceedings of the Annual Meeting of the Cognitive Science Society*, volume 36.

Jey Han Lau, Alexander Clark, and Shalom Lappin. 2015. Unsupervised prediction of acceptability judgements. In *Proceedings of the 53rd Annual Meeting of the Association for Computational Linguistics and the 7th International Joint Conference on Natural Language Processing (Volume 1: Long Papers)*, pages 1618–1628.

Brian MacWhinney. 2017. A shared platform for studying second language acquisition. *Language Learning*, 67(S1):254–275.

Emma Marsden, Luke Plonsky, A Gudmestad, and A Edmonds. 2018. Data, open science, and methodological reform in second language acquisition research. *Critical reflections on data in second language acquisition*, 51:219–228.

Beéta Megyesi, Lena Granstedt, Sofia Johansson, Julia Prentice, Dan Rosén, Carl-Johan Schenström, Gunlög Sundberg, Mats Wirén, and Elena Volodina. 2018. Learner corpus anonymization in the age of gdpr: Insights from the creation of a learner corpus of swedish. In *Proceedings of the 7th Workshop on NLP for Computer Assisted Language Learning (NLP4CALL 2018) at SLTC, Stockholm, 7th November 2018*, 152, pages 47–56. Linköping University Electronic Press.

Lisa Rudebeck and Gunlög Sundberg. 2020. Correction annotation guidelines. SweLL project. Technical report.

Elena Volodina, Lena Granstedt, Arild Matsson, Beáta Megyesi, Ildikó Pilán, Julia Prentice, Dan Rosén, Lisa Rudebeck, Carl-Johan Schenström, Gunlög Sundberg, et al. 2019. The SweLL Language Learner Corpus: From Design to Annotation. *Northern European Journal of Language Technology*, 6:67–104.

Elena Volodina, Yousuf Ali Mohammed, Sandra Derbring, Arild Matsson, and Beáta Megyesi. 2020. Towards privacy by design in learner corpora research: A case of on-the-fly pseudonymization of swedish learner essays. In *Proceedings of the 28th International Conference on Computational Linguistics*, pages 357–369.

Elena Volodina, Ildikó Pilán, Stian Rødven Eide, and Hannes Heidarsson. 2014. You get what you annotate: a pedagogically annotated corpus of coursebooks for Swedish as a Second Language. In *Proceedings of the third workshop on NLP for computer-assisted language learning*, pages 128–144.

Joachim Wagner, Jennifer Foster, Josef van Genabith, et al. 2009. Judging grammaticality: Experiments in sentence classification. *Calico Journal*, 26(3):474–490.

Alex Wang, Yada Pruksachatkun, Nikita Nangia, Amanpreet Singh, Julian Michael, Felix Hill, Omer Levy, and Samuel R Bowman. 2019. Superglue: A stickier benchmark for general-purpose language understanding systems. *arXiv preprint arXiv:1905.00537*.

Alex Wang, Amanpreet Singh, Julian Michael, Felix Hill, Omer Levy, and Samuel R Bowman. 2018. GLUE: A multi-task benchmark and analysis platform for natural language understanding. *arXiv preprint arXiv:1804.07461*.

Alex Warstadt, Amanpreet Singh, and Samuel R Bowman. 2019. Neural network acceptability judgments. *Transactions of the Association for Computational Linguistics*, 7:625–641.

Mark D Wilkinson, Michel Dumontier, IJsbrand Jan Aalbersberg, Gabrielle Appleton, Myles Axton, Arie Baak, Niklas Blomberg, Jan-Willem Boiten, Luiz Bonino da Silva Santos, Philip E Bourne, et al. 2016. The FAIR Guiding Principles for scientific data management and stewardship. *Scientific data*, 3(1):1–9.

Appendices

Appendix A. Overview of all correction types in the source corpus

Categories	Explanation	A-lev	B-lev	C-lev	Total
Orthography (3 codes)					*4381*
O	Spelling error	1746	754	769	3269
O-Cap	Upper / lower case	264	73	229	566
O-Comp	Problem with compounding	252	62	232	546
Lexical level (4 codes)					*4876*
L-Der	Word formation problem (derivation or compounding)	193	124	404	721
L-FL	Non-Swedish word corrected to Swedish word	46	17	26	89
L-Ref	Choice of anaphoric expression	214	112	298	624
L-W	Wrong word or phrase	1157	562	1723	3442
Morphological level (8 codes)					*8005*
M-Adj/adv	Adjective word form corrected to adverb form	45	13	46	104
M-Case	Nominative vs genitive / accusative cases	46	64	147	257
M-Def	Definiteness: articles; form of nouns and adjectives	1056	362	1550	2968
M-F	Grammatical category changed, form kept	168	50	82	300
M-Gend	Gender problem (neuter / uter)	370	131	452	953
M-Num	Number problem (plural / singular)	351	157	523	1031
M-Other	Other corrections, incl. comparative forms of adjectives	55	28	33	116
M-Verb	Verb forms; auxiliaries	984	489	803	2276

Figure 2: Overview of all correction types in the SweLL corpus, part 1

Syntactical level (11 codes)					*7696*
S-Adv	Word order: Adverbial placement	235	131	419	785
S-Comp	Compound vs multi-word expressions; lex-synt restructuring	32	8	96	136
S-Clause	Change of basic clause structure; synt function of components	387	210	532	1129
S-Ext	Extensive and complex correction / restructuring	133	65	112	310
S-FinV	Word order: Finite verb placement	283	142	276	701
S-M	Word missing (i.e. added in the target)	719	375	810	1904
S-Msubj	Subject missing (i.e. added in the target)	175	74	185	434
S-Other	Other syntactical correction	20	20	40	80
S-R	Word redundant (i.e. removed in the target)	501	235	687	1423
S-Type	Change of phrase type / part of speech	209	111	275	595
S-WO	Word order: other	67	40	92	199
Punctuation (4 codes)					*1834*
P-M	Punctuation missing (added in the target)	643	312	879	1834
P-R	Punctuation redundant (removed in the target)	133	85	226	444
P-Sent	Sentence segmentation	6	7	26	39
P-W	Wrong punctuation	127	66	244	437
Other (5 codes)					*1573*
C	Consistency correction, necessitated by another correction	397	205	606	1208
Cit-FL	Non-Swedish word kept (i.e. no correction in the target)	14	0	40	54
Com!	Comments for the corpus users	50	1	58	109
OBS!	Internal temporary comments to annotators	9	7	49	65
X	Unintelligible string	93	27	17	137
TOTAL					*29 285*

Figure 3: Overview of all correction types in the SweLL corpus, part 2

Using Broad Linguistic Complexity Modeling for Cross-Lingual Readability Assessment

Zarah Weiss, Xiaobin Chen, Detmar Meurers
Department of Linguistics & LEAD Graduate School
University of Tübingen
Germany
{zweiss,xchen,dm}@sfs.uni-tuebingen.de

Abstract

We investigate the readability classification of English and German reading materials for language learners based on a broad linguistic complexity feature set supporting the parallel analysis of both German and English. After illustrating the quality of the feature set by showing that it yields state-of-the-art classification performance for the established OneStopEnglish corpus (Vajjala and Lučić, 2018), we introduce the Spotlight corpus. This new data set contains graded reading materials produced by the same publisher for English and German, which supports an analysis comparing the linguistic characteristics of texts at different reading levels across languages. As far as we are aware, this is both the first readability corpus for German L2 learners, as well as the first corpus with comparably classified reading material for learners across multiple languages.

After discussing the first results for a readability classifier for German L2 learners, we show that the linguistic complexity analyses for the cross-language experiments identify features successfully characterizing the readability of texts for language learners across languages, as well as some language-specific characteristics of different reading levels.

1 Introduction

The language input available to language learners is a driving force for Second Language Acquisition (SLA), and reading is an important source of language input. Material that is just above the level of the learner is assumed to be best for fostering learning, which depending on the SLA tradition is characterized as i+1 input of Krashen (1981), input in the Zone of Proximal Development in socio-cultural approaches (Lantolf et al., 2015), or input reflecting second language development in usage-based SLA approaches (Ellis and Collins, 2009). Note that the focus here is not just on input that is understandable and of interest to the learner but also rich in developmentally proximal language properties.

This dependency of readability on reading purpose and individual language skills makes the identification of appropriate reading materials a major challenge for educators, especially for heterogeneous learning groups. Automatic readability assessment may facilitate the retrieval of appropriate reading materials for individual language learners. It refers to the task of identifying texts that are suitable for a given group of target readers with a specific reading purpose (Collins-Thompson, 2014). Recent approaches to automatic readability assessment also investigate the use of neural networks (Martinc et al., 2019). However, the identification of linguistic characteristics that impact the readability of texts in itself can also yield valuable insights for education, because it may inform content creators of reading materials for language learning. This also is an interesting research endeavor from a linguistic perspective and speaks against solely focusing on neural approaches. Similarly, it remains to be investigated to which extent these linguistic characteristics may generalize across languages given comparable target groups and reading purposes.

While there has been a considerable amount of work on automatic readability assessment for English, there is still insufficient research on other

Zarah Weiss, Xiaobin Chen and Detmar Meurers 2021. Using broad linguistic complexity modeling for cross-lingual readability assessment. *Proceedings of the 10th Workshop on Natural Language Processing for Computer Assisted Language Learning (NLP4CALL 2021)*. Linköping Electronic Conference Proceedings 177: 38–54.

languages. The lack of suitable training corpora for other languages remains as one major limiting factor (Collins-Thompson, 2014), despite some research efforts to facilitate unsupervised readability assessments (Benzahra and François, 2019; Martinc et al., 2019). For example, there has been some recent work on German readability classifiers for native speakers (Weiss and Meurers, 2018; Weiss et al., 2018; Dittrich et al., 2019). Yet, a lack of corpus resources has so far hindered the development of a readability classifier for German as a second or foreign language (L2) learners.

In this article, we introduce a novel cross-lingual feature collection for broad linguistic modeling of German and English complexity. Although neural classification approaches have been strongly represented in readability assessment, our literature review (see Section 2) shows that their success has been very much limited on the benchmark data we use for this study and fallen behind the feature-based readability classification approaches which are also providing deeper linguistic insights while requiring less computational power.[1] However, while broad feature collections for language-specific complexity modeling have been proposed for English (Chen and Meurers, 2019) and German (Weiss and Meurers, 2018), they are not applicable across languages. This has so far hindered the cross-lingual study of similarities between characteristics of readability. We first validate our approach by applying it to an established readability corpus for English (Vajjala and Lučić, 2018), before using it to train two readability classifiers for labeling English and German L2 reading materials resulting in the first readability classifier of this kind for German. For this, we introduce a novel data set of English and German reading materials for beginning, intermediate, and advanced learners of English and German, the Spotlight corpus. We address the following research questions:

1. Can we train a successful readability classifier for German and for English using broad complexity modeling?
2. Can these classifiers generalize beyond their training language to cross-lingual contexts?
3. Which linguistic features are relevant for the distinction of reading levels and how do they differ between English and German?

The article is structured as follows. First, we discuss related work on readability assessment of English and German (Section 2). Then, we introduce the novel Spotlight data set (Section 3.1) as well as the OneStopEnglish corpus (Section 3.2) which we use as benchmark data set. We proceed to introduce our approach to automatic complexity assessment and the feature set (Section 4) we use throughout our machine learning experiments (Sections 5 and 6). Finally, we compare the informativeness of individual complexity features on Spotlight for the discrimination of reading levels (Section 7) before we come to the conclusion (Section 8) and outlook (Section 9).

2 Related Work

Automatic readability assessment has a long history dating back to the first readability formulas developed in the early 20th century, see DuBay (2006) for an overview. Traditional readability formulas employ few surface text characteristics such as text, sentence, and word length (Flesch, 1948; Dale and Chall, 1948). They are still widely used especially in non-linguistic studies on web accessibility (Esfahani et al., 2016; Grootens-Wiegers et al., 2015), in information retrieval systems (Miltsakaki and Troutt, 2007; Chinkina et al., 2016), and for confirming the compliance of reading materials with specific accessibility guidelines (Weiss et al., 2018; Yaneva et al., 2016), such as Easy-to-Read materials.[2]

Over the last two decades, there has been a shift towards computational readability classification approaches based on machine learning techniques employing feature engineering with Natural Language Processing (NLP) methods, see Collins-Thompson (2014) and Benjamin (2012) for an overview. Among others, linguistic complexity features from SLA research (Vajjala and Meurers, 2012), word frequency measures (Chen and Meurers, 2017), and features of text cohesion (Crossley et al., 2017) from Writing Quality Assessment research (Crossley, 2020) were shown to be valuable features for readabilty assessemnt.

While most readability research focuses on English (Collins-Thompson, 2014), to a lesser degree these approaches have also been employed for other languages such as Russian (Reynolds, 2016),

[1] See Strubell et al. (2019) for a discussion of the considerable energy demands of deep learning approaches in NLP.

[2] https://www.inclusion-europe.eu/easy-to-read/

French (François and Fairon, 2012), Swedish (Pilán et al., 2015), Italian (Dell'Orletta et al., 2013), or German (Vor der Brück and Hartrumpf, 2007). For German, the most recent classification approach has been proposed by Weiss and Meurers (2018) who use broad linguistic complexity modeling of German to distinguish between German media texts targeting adults and children. However, this approach only provides a rather coarse binary distinction and identifies reading materials for information retrieval (i.e., with a focus on accessibility), rather than language learning (i.e., with a focus on challenging the reader's language competence). Given the lack of appropriate multi-level reading corpora, so far no classifiers for German L2 readers have been trained.

Recently, several neural network approaches have been proposed for readability assessment (Martinc et al., 2019; Madrazo Azpiazu and Pera, 2019). Martinc et al. (2019) investigate the performance of supervised and unsupervised neural readability classification approaches for English and Slovenian. They find that their neural approaches perform overall at the state-of-the art level of feature-based classification approaches in both languages. For the OneStopEnglish corpus, their best classifier reaches an accuracy of 78.71% which performs at the same level as the feature-based classifier reported by Vajjala and Lučić (2018) with an accuracy of 78.12%. With this, the performance of neural approaches on OneStopEnglish does not exceed the original benchmark and lies substantially below the current state-of-the art on this data set, which is held by a feature-based classifier with an accuracy of 90.09% (Bengoetxea et al., 2020). In other words, while neural classification approaches have been very successful in several NLP tasks, they are currently not competitive with the breadth and depth of analyses supported by feature-based approaches to readability classification.

Only little research has been conducted on multilingual readability classification. While there are some neural classification approaches that are developed to be applicable across languages (Martinc et al., 2019; Madrazo Azpiazu and Pera, 2019), feature-based approaches are usually language-specific. An exception is the study by De Clercq and Hoste (2016), who compare the informativeness of lexical, semantic and syntactic features for English and Dutch readability classification. The cross-lingual applicability of multilingual models has so far not been investigated, except for a series of studies by Madrazo Azpiazu and Pera on the VikiWiki corpus, which distinguishes simplified Vikidia.org texts for 8 to 13 year old children from regular Wikipedia.org texts for Basque, Catalan, Dutch, English, French, Italian, and Spanish.[3] On this data, Madrazo Azpiazu and Pera (2020a) investigate the transferablility of the neural readability classification approach by Madrazo Azpiazu and Pera (2019). They demonstrate that training on multilingual data sets may improve readability classification results for low-resource languages in the binary classification task. Madrazo Azpiazu and Pera (2020b) follow a similar approach using a feature-based readability classification approach based on shallow features, morphological features, syntactic features, and semantic features. They report similar results as Madrazo Azpiazu and Pera (2020a). While these studies make an important first contribution to the assessment of cross-lingual readability assessment, they are clearly limited by the binary distinction of simplified texts for children and regular Wikipedia texts. The success of transfer learning for more fine-grained and practically relevant readability level distinctions remains to be empirically determined.

3 Data

3.1 Spotlight corpus

The Spotlight corpus consists of articles from the two monthly language learning magazines *Spotlight*[4] for adult German learners of English and *Deutsch perfekt*[5] for adult language learners of German. Both magazines are published by *Spotlight Verlag*, a leading European publisher for foreign language learning materials.[6] The magazines contain reading materials for beginning, intermediate, and advanced language learners which the publisher equates with the Common European Framework of Reference (CEFR) levels A2 (level: easy), B1/B2 (level: medium) and C1 (level: advanced).

We extracted all articles from the PDF versions of the respective issues provided to us for research purposes by the publisher.The type setting of the magazines made it impossible to di-

[3]https://github.com/ionmadrazo/VikiWiki

[4]https://www.spotlight-online.de

[5]https://www.deutsch-perfekt.com

[6]https://www.spotlight-verlag.de

rectly extract the individual articles with a PDF converter without loosing the information of their reading level. Instead, we manually identified and extracted each article using screenshots which we then converted to plain text using Google's optical character recognition (OCR) API.[7] This way, we extracted the English subset (henceforth Spotlight-EN) from the 110 issues of the *Spotlight* magazine that were published from January 2012 to December 2019 and the German subset (henceforth Spotlight-DE) from the 45 issues of the *Deutsch perfekt* magazine published from January 2018 to December 2019 (see corpus profiles in Table 1). The imbalance of readability levels in both data sets is due to the imbalanced distribution of reading levels in both magazines.

Level	N. docs	N. sents	N. words
Spotlight-EN			
Easy	1.030	13.921	212.267
Medium	1.528	60.232	898.695
Advanced	1.030	24.288	440.793
$\sum$	3.285	98.441	1.551.755
Spotlight-DE			
Easy	763	16.135	180.178
Medium	509	27.107	338.553
Advanced	174	11.713	155.160
$\sum$	1.446	54.955	673.891

Table 1: Corpus profiles for Spotlight data

It is noteworthy that in both magazines, articles may vary considerably in length irrespective of their reading level. This is shown in Table 2. The table showcases that number of words – which has been and continues to be a popular surface feature for readability classification – is not sufficient to distinguish reading levels in this data set.

3.2 OneStopEnglish corpus

The OneStopEnglish (OSE) corpus by Vajjala and Lučić (2018) consists of overall 567 Guardian news paper articles that were rewritten for adult English as a Second Language learners by MacMillan Education.[8] Each Guardian article is available in an elementary (ele), intermediate (int), and advanced (adv) version resulting in a perfectly balanced corpus.[9] The OSE corpus is a by now established reference data set for studies related to readability assessment and text simplification (Bengoetxea et al., 2020; Benzahra and François, 2019). Currently, the best results reported for OSE achieve an accuracy of 90.09% in a feature-based machine learning approach by Bengoetxea et al. (2020). Table 3 shows the corpus profile of the OSE data set. Table 4 displays the differences of article length across reading levels in OSE.[10]

[7]https://cloud.google.com/vision

[8]https://www.onestopenglish.com

	$\mu \pm SD$	M	Min	Max
Spotlight-EN				
Easy	206±166	137	53	877
Medium	588±555	493	23	4.497
Advanced	606±509	489	26	2.940
Spotlight-DE				
Easy	236±235	137	60	1.469
Medium	665±769	448	72	5.605
Advanced	892±537	524	91	4.161

Table 2: Article length in words in Spotlight data ($\mu \pm SD$= mean ± standard deviation; M = median; Min = minimal; Max = maximal)

Level	N. docs	N. sents	N. words
Ele.	189	6.033	105.169
Int.	189	6.634	128.335
Adv.	189	7.221	162.449
$\sum$	567	19.888	395.953

Table 3: Corpus profile for OSE

Level	$\mu(\pm SD)$	M	Min	Max
Ele.	556(±109)	561	267	948
Int.	679(±117)	691	315	1.083
Adv.	860(±171)	857	357	1.465

Table 4: Article length in words in OSE ($\mu \pm SD$= mean ± standard deviation; M = median; Min = minimal; Max = maximal)

[9]Since the three OneStopEnglish levels (elementary, intermediate, advanced) are not explicitly aligned with the CEFR levels, used to characterize the Spotlight levels (easy=A2, medium=B, advanced=C1), we keep the labels separate throughout the article.

[10]The numbers reported here slightly deviate from those reported by Vajjala and Lučić (2018), due to minor differences in the automatic tokenization.

As also noted by Vajjala and Lučić (2018, p. 299), there is a general tendency of articles becoming longer with increasing reading level. However, note the standard deviation of the article length within reading levels, which is considerable despite being much lower than the variability displayed in the Spotlight data.

4 Automatic Complexity Analysis

4.1 Complexity Features

We calculate 312 features of linguistic complexity merging the feature collections proposed by us in our previous work on German (Weiss and Meurers, 2018) and English (Chen, 2018). These have been successfully used for the tasks of readability assessment (Chen and Meurers, 2018; Weiss and Meurers, 2018; Kühberger et al., 2019), second language proficiency assessment (Weiss and Meurers, 2019b, 2021), academic language proficiency (Weiss and Meurers, 2019a), and teachers' grading objectivity (Weiss et al., 2019). While each of the feature collections contains more language-specific features than the joined feature collection proposed in this work, this is as far as we are aware the broadest collection of complexity features applicable to both, English and German, thus facilitating cross-lingual comparisons of complexity.

Our broad set of cross-lingual complexity features covers the theoretical linguistic domains of syntax, lexicon, and morphology, as well as features of discourse cohesion and psycho-linguistic features of human language use and human language processing. It also includes some surface measures from or inspired by classic readability formulas.

4.1.1 Surface Length (LEN)

We measure 21 surface text length features inspired by traditional readability formulas. They measure the raw number of sentences, syllables, letters, (unique) words including and excluding punctuation marks and numbers, and (unique) tokens. It also includes mean and standard deviations of sentence length and word length measured in letters, syllables, and words as well as the mean and standard deviation of words with more than two syllables. These categories can be applied without language-specific adjustments, except for the identification of syllables which are based on language-specific regular expressions.

4.1.2 Syntactic Complexity (SYN)

We assess several features of clausal and phrasal complexity that have been proposed in the SLA complexity literature (Wolfe-Quintero et al., 1998; Kyle, 2016) inspired by the implementations by Chen (2018) and Weiss and Meurers (2021). We measure 20 features of clausal elaborateness. This includes features measuring the length of clauses and (complex) t-units in various units (such as words, syllables, letters), as well as features of clausal coordination and subordination, such as the number of relative or dependent clauses per clause.

Furthermore, we measure 28 features of phrasal elaborateness. This includes several features focusing on the complexity of noun phrases (NPs) including the number of pre- and postnominal modifiers per complex NP, the number of (complex) NPs per clause, t-unit and sentence, and the length of NPs in words. It also entails features measuring the complexity of verb phrases (VPs) including the number of verb clusters and VPs per clause, t-unit and sentence and the length of verb clusters in words. We also measure the complexity of prepositional phrases (PPs) such as the number of (complex) PPs per clause, t-unit and sentence or the length of PPs in words. Finally, this includes measures of coordinate phrases per clause, t-unit and sentence.

While these syntactic features are identified based on language-specific TregEx (Levy and Andrew, 2006) patterns for constituency trees, we carefully designed all extraction rules to yield equivalent results across languages.

We also measure syntactic variation based on 12 measures of parse tree edit distances following Chen (2018).

4.1.3 Lexical Complexity (LEX)

We measure several complexity features assessing lexical richness, variation, and density that have been proposed in the SLA complexity literature (Wolfe-Quintero et al., 1998) inspired by the implementations by Chen (2018) and Weiss and Meurers (2021). These can be applied straight forward across languages as long as similar word categories (such as adjectives, nouns, verbs, etc.) can be identified.

This feature set includes 27 features of lexical density including POS-based lexical density features as well as 9 features of lexical diversity including lexical word, verb, noun, adjective, and adverb variation. Finally, we assess 53 features of lexical richness including several mathematical transformations of type token ratios (TTR), parts-of-speech specific TTRs, the Uber index and HD-D (McCarthy and Jarvis, 2007).

4.1.4 Morphological Complexity (MOR)

Morphological complexity has been argued to be an important feature for readability assessment of morphological richer languages than English, such as German (Hancke et al., 2012; Weiss and Meurers, 2018) or Basque (Gonzalez-Dios et al., 2014). However, few measures have been used in readability assessment that are applicable across languages with different morphological systems. We use the Morphological Complexity Index (MCI) proposed by Brezina and Pallotti (2019) to assess morphological complexity independent of language by measuring the variability of morphological exponents of specific parts-of-speech within a text. These morphological exponents can be identified by contrasting word forms with their stems which makes the features applicable across languages. We assess overall 40 MCI features for verbs, nouns, and adjectives based on different number of samples and sampling sizes with and without repetition.

4.1.5 Discourse Cohesion (DIS)

We assess 26 features measuring the mean overlap of word forms and lemmas of lexical words, nouns, and grammatical arguments between sentences as well as their standard deviation. Each feature is calculated locally (between neighboring sentences) and globally (across all sentences in the text). These implicit cohesion features were originally proposed in CohMetrix (McNamara et al., 2014). Unlike explicit cohesion measures, such as the number of particular connectives, they are directly applicable across languages.

4.1.6 Language Use (USE)

Word frequency features have a long tradition in both, readability and complexity research. Yet, word frequencies obtained from different frequency data bases are not necessarily comparable. We address this issue by using the SUBTLEX-US (Brysbaert et al., 2011b) and SUBTLEX-DE (Brysbaert et al., 2011a) frequency data bases. We consider both SUBTLEX frequency data bases equivalent for the purposes of our complexity analysis because they represent word frequencies from the same register and were created to be maximally comparable. To mitigate effects due to the different sizes of the underlying corpora, we only use word frequencies per million words.

Based on this, we calculate 56 word frequency features including the mean (log) frequency of all words, lexical words, and function words and their standard deviations as well as frequencies for verbs, nouns, adjectives, and adverbs.

4.1.7 Human Language Processing (HLP)

Weiss and Meurers (2018) have proposed to use features based on theories explaining human sentence processing difficulties for readability assessment. They propose features based on the Dependency Locality Theory (Gibson, 2000) using the different integration cost weight configurations proposed in Shain et al. (2016). While the psycholinguistic theories have been formulated for English, the complexity features by Weiss and Meurers (2018) have so far not been applied for complexity modeling beyond German.

We implemented 21 features for both, English and German, based on universal dependencies to make them applicable across languages. These features calculate the average, maximal and highest adjacent discourse integration costs per finite verb across different weight configurations.

4.2 NLP Pipeline

We calculate our complexity features following a three-step procedure. First, we run a pipeline of Natural Language Processing (NLP) tools to provide linguistic annotations for the data. The annotation pipeline primarily relies on Stanford CoreNLP (Manning et al., 2014) which we use for sentence segmentation, tokenization, parts-of-speech (POS) tagging, constituency parsing, and dependency parsing for English and German. We additionally employ the Mate tools (Bohnet and Nivre, 2012) for lemmatization, because CoreNLP only provides a lemmatizer for English but not for German. We also use the OpenNLP Snowball stemmer to extract stems for English and German. For all annotations, we use the respective default models provided with the NLP tools.

Second, we count linguistic constructs using a set of extraction rules as well as word frequencies. This procedure is fully identical across languages except for syllable counts, POS-based counts, and syntactic complexity counts which we designed to be comparable across languages as described in the previous section. For all other features we use identical extraction rules.

Third, we calculate a variety of complexity feature ratios based on these counts. This step is fully language independent.

4.3 Feature Extraction and Selection

We extracted all 312 features on OSE, Spotlight-EN and Spotlight-DE as described in the previous subsection. We then identified all features that were not variable on any of the three data sets. This way, we could exclude features that are irrelevant for the data sets while keeping the feature collections comparable across data sets. For this, we removed all features for which the most common feature value across all three data sets occurred in 95% of the data or more.

The feature removal reduced the entire feature collection to 301 features. Only human language processing features were removed through this step, including all features measuring high adjacent integration costs.

5 Establishing our Approach on OSE

5.1 Set-up

To validate the performance of our feature-based readability classification approach against an established benchmark data set, we first trained a classifier to predict reading levels on the OSE data. For this, we used the 301 complexity features from Section 4.3. All feature values were z-transformed and centered around zero. We trained a random forest (RF), an ordinal RF, a Support Vector Machine (SVM) with a radial kernel, and a SVM with a polynomial kernel in R (R Core Team, 2015) using the `caret` package (Kuhn, 2020).[11] In the following, we only report the results for the SVM using a polynomial kernel, which outperformed the other algorithms.[12]

To not reduce the relatively small data set further, we train and test using 10-folds cross-validation. We compare the performance of the classifier on OSE with a) the random accuracy baseline of 33.3% and b) the state-of-the art performance on this data set by Bengoetxea et al. (2020), reaching 90.09%. We also report the individual precision, recall and F1 scores for each reading level.

5.2 Results

The OSE classifier reaches an accuracy of 92.06% with a 95% confidence interval (CI) $= [89.52\%, 94.15\%]$ in 10-folds cross-validation. This significantly outperforms the random baseline of 33.33% (p-Value $< 2 \cdot 10^{-16}$).[13] It also exceeds the results of Bengoetxea et al. (2020).

Table 5 displays the confusion matrix for the classification summed across all 10-folds.

Pred\Obs.	Ele.	Int.	Adv.
Ele.	179	9	4
Int.	9	173	15
Adv.	1	7	170

Table 5: Confusion matrix: OSE 10-CV

It shows that misclassifications occur predominantly at adjacent reading levels and that there does not seem to be any systematic bias. Table 6 reports precision, recall, and F1 score per level. The performance across reading levels is relatively balanced. Elementary texts have a slightly higher recall, while advanced texts have a higher precision. As expected when comparing an ordinal classification level with two adjacent levels with levels with only one adjacent level, intermediate texts receive the lowest scores for precision and recall.

	Ele.	Int.	Adv.
Precision	93.2	87.8	95.5
Recall	94.7	91.5	90.0
F1	94.0	89.6	92.6

Table 6: Performance for OSE 10-CV

6 Classifying Readability on Spotlight

6.1 Set-up

After establishing the performance of our approach against the OSE benchmark data set, we turn to our main research question, which compares feature-based readability classification across languages on Spotlight-EN for English and Spotlight-DE for German. Our classification is

[11] All R scripts, data tables, and trained models that are being reported in this and the following sections are publicly available on OSF at https://osf.io/5hbcs/

[12] SVM parameters: degree = 3, scale = 0.001, and C = 1.

[13] Here and throughout the article we report p-values obtained with one-sided t-tests with $H_1 = Acc. > Baseline.$

again based on the 301 complexity features we extracted and identified following the procedure described in Section 4.3. All feature values were z-transformed and centered around zero separately for Spotlight-EN and Spotlight-DE. This way, the classifiers are learning based on the standard deviations from the data sets' mean values rather than the raw feature values. This was supposed to mitigate language-specific differences, for example, regarding the average sentence length in German and English.

The set-up of the classification experiment is identical to the one described in Section 5.1. In the following, we only report the results for the ordinal RF which outperformed the other algorithms on both Spotlight data sets.[14] Since this is a novel data set, we use the majority baseline as sole reference to evaluate the classifier performance in the within language condition (Section 6.2.1).

For our cross-language classification experiment (Section 6.2.2), we apply the previously trained classifiers to the respective other subset of the Spotlight data, i.e., testing on Spotlight-DE for the classifier trained on Spotlight-EN and vice versa. Unlike previous cross-linguistic readability classification approaches that used cross-lingual data to augment limited training resources, this set-up tests the generalization of our classifiers in a form of zero-shot learning. We again compare the performance of each classifier across-languages against the majority baseline on the respective testing data and the within-language classification performance.

We also report the individual precision, recall and F1 scores for each reading level throughout all classification experiments.

6.2 Results

6.2.1 Within-language Performance

Table 7 displays the results of all four classification experiments on the Spotlight data. The Spotlight-EN classifier reaches an accuracy of 74.5% in 10-folds cross-validation. This significantly outperforms the majority baseline of 46.5% (p-Value $< 2.2 \cdot 10^{-16}$).

Looking at the confusion matrix in Table 8, we see that the classification is relatively balanced, even though in proportion to their total count advanced texts are classified incorrectly more often than the other reading levels. This can also be seen in the relatively low F1 score for advanced texts displayed in the first three rows of Table 10.

The Spotlight-DE classifier reaches an accuracy of 88.0% in 10-folds cross-validation. This significantly outperforms the majority baseline of 52.8% (p-Value $< 2.2 \cdot 10^{-16}$). Table 9 shows the confusion matrix for the classification, which shows good classification results throughout all reading levels. This is mirrored in the high precision and recall scores displayed in rows four to six in Table 10.

6.2.2 Cross-language Performance

For the classification across languages, the Spotlight-EN classifier reaches an accuracy of 55.5% on Spotlight-DE. Although this performance is considerably worse than for the within-language classification, this significantly outperforms the majority baseline of 52.8% (p-Value = 0.02118) showing that the classifier somewhat generalizes beyond English even if the performance drops considerably. Looking at the confusion matrix in Table 11, one of the most common misclassifications is the labeling of easy texts as medium. The classifier overestimates the reading difficulty of many easy and medium texts. This results in a high precision but low recall for easy texts, as shown in rows seven to nine in Table 10.

The Spotlight-DE classifier reaches an accuracy of 53.4% on Spotlight-EN. Again, this is much worse than the results for the within-language classification, but significantly outperforms the majority baseline of 46.51% (p-Value $= 1.284 \cdot 10^{-15}$). This shows again that the classifier generalizes to some degree in the zero-shot learning scenario. Looking at the confusion matrix in Table 12, it can be seen that the classifier tends to underestimate the reading difficulty of advanced texts (classifying them as medium or even easy) and of medium texts (classifying them as easy). This results in a relatively high recall for easy texts and very low recall for advanced texts, as shown in the final three rows in Table 10.

6.3 Discussion

The two readability classifiers trained on Spotlight-EN and Spotlight-DE are highly successful when applied within their training language and exceed the majority baseline con-

[14] Parameters for the English model: number of sets = 50, number of trees per div. = 150, number of final trees = 600; parameters for the German model: number of sets = 150, number of trees per div. = 150, number of final trees = 200.

Train	Test	Acc.	95% CI	Maj.	Acc. < Maj.
Spotlight-EN	10-folds CV	74.5	$[73.0, 76.0]$	46.5	$< 2.2 \cdot 10^{-16}$
Spotlight-DE	10-folds CV	88.0	$[86.1, 89.6]$	52.8	$< 2.2 \cdot 10^{-16}$
Spotlight-EN	Spotlight-DE	55.5	$[52.9, 58.1]$	52.8	.02118
Spotlight-DE	Spotlight-EN	53.4	$[51.7, 55.1]$	46.5	$1.284 \cdot 10^{-15}$

Table 7: Overall classifier accuracy (Acc.) on Spotlight data compared against majority baseline (Maj.)

Pred\Obs.	Easy	Medium	Advanced
Easy	816	171	37
Medium	208	1,210	268
Advanced	6	147	422

Table 8: Confusion matrix Spotlight-EN 10-CV

Pred\Obs.	Easy	Medium	Advanced
Easy	727	83	1
Medium	34	399	27
Advanced	2	27	146

Table 9: Confusion matrix Spotlight-DE 10-CV

	Easy	Medium	Advanced
Spotlight-EN 10 CV			
Precision	79.7	71.8	73.4
Recall	79.2	79.2	58.1
F1.	79.5	75.3	65.0
Spotlight-DE 10 CV			
Precision	89.6	86.7	83.4
Recall	95.3	78.4	83.9
F1.	92.4	82.4	83.7
Spotlight-EN on Spotlight-DE			
Precision	82.3	42.5	52.4
Recall	44.6	67.4	67.8
F1.	57.8	52.1	59.2
Spotlight-DE on Spotlight-EN			
Precision	49.3	59.0	53.4
Recall	80.3	47.9	27.0
F1.	61.1	52.9	35.8

Table 10: Level-wise performance on Spotlight

Pred\Obs.	Easy	Medium	Advanced
Easy	341	73	0
Medium	408	343	56
Advanced	14	93	118

Table 11: Confusion matrix Spotlight-EN on Spotlight-DE

Pred\Obs.	Easy	Medium	Advanced
Easy	827	635	216
Medium	193	732	315
Advanced	10	161	196

Table 12: Confusion matrix Spotlight-DE on Spotlight-EN

siderably. When comparing the performance of the Spotlight-EN classifier and the OSE classifier, the different nature of the two English corpora has to be taken into account. OSE consists of the same 189 articles simplified for three different reading levels, which is a somewhat artificial set-up for training data. The Spotlight-EN corpus, instead, consists of different texts specifically written for a given reading level which is closer to real-life texts for which language learners might require automatic readability ratings. Thus, we consider the within-language performance of the Spotlight-EN classifier satisfactory.

For the Spotlight-DE classifier, we observe a very high performance throughout reading levels. Spotlight-DE is the first data set for the readability assessment of texts for German L2 learners that allows a distinction for beginning, intermediate, and advanced learners of German. Thus, we cannot compare the performance to a reference corpus or cross-corpus test the Spotlight-DE classifier. Overall, the classification results are sufficient to use the Spotlight-DE classifier in real-life scenarios, even though a cross-corpus evaluation on a comparable data set would be ideal to confirm its generalizability as soon as such a data set becomes available.

Turning to our cross-language classification experiments, we find that both classifiers generalize to some extent in the zero-shot learning scenarios, despite considerable drops in performance. This result is not to be taken for granted due to the linguistic differences between English and German. These are highly promising initial results. Further research is needed to investigate to which extent this generalization also applies across other languages.

The comparison of the confusion matrices of both cross-lingual classification experiments reveals a symmetrical regularity in the misclassifications. While the German classifier underestimates the reading levels of the English texts, the English classifier tends to overestimate the readability of the German texts. Since the classifiers are trained and tested on feature z-scores centered around the mean this behavior is not immediately expected and warrants further investigation in future research.

Group	EN (%)		DE (%)		All
LEN	7	(33.3)	5	(23.8)	21
USE	17	(30.4)	11	(19.6)	56
LEX Density	7	(15.9)	5	(18.5)	27
LEX Diversity	1	(11.1)	1	(11.1)	9
LEX Richness	4	(7.5)	5	(9.4)	53
SYN Clausal	1	(5.0)	8	(40.0)	20
SYN Phrasal	1	(3.6)	5	(17.9)	28
SYN Variation	2	(16.7)	0	(0.0)	12
MOR	7	(17.5)	3	(7.5)	40
DIS	2	(8.2)	0	(0.0)	24
HLP	0	(0.0)	0	(0.0)	11
$\sum$	49	(16.3)	43	(14.3)	301

Table 13: Informative features selected on Spotlight-EN (EN), Spotlight-DE (DE), and the total number of features in the group (All)

7 Feature Informativeness on Spotlight

7.1 Set-up

To identify which of the 301 complexity features identified in Section 4.3 are most informative for the readability classification, we identify the most informative features using the correlation-based feature subset selection for machine learning approach by Hall (1999). This method identifies the subset of features that exhibits the highest correlation with the class to be predicted (in our case reading level) while minimizing the intercorrelation of features within the subset. We use the implementation provided in the WEKA toolkit version 3.9.5 (Hall et al., 2009) for feature identification. We report the percentage of features selected across each feature group before we discuss in more detail the intersection of features in both data sets.

7.2 Results

Table 13 displayed the raw number and percentage of features selected on Spotlight-EN and Spotlight-DE across feature groups and the total number of features contained in the feature group. To make the result summary more interpretable, we split syntactic and lexical complexity features into the individual subgroups distinguished within Sections 4.1.2 and 4.1.3. A full list of all features that are informative on either data set is displayed in Appendix A. Figure 1 shows the boxplots of all features that were selected for Spotlight-EN as well as Spotlight-DE.

On Spotlight-EN and on Spotlight-DE, up to a third of all surface length features are selected, most of which are informative on both data sets. All of the shared length features increase with reading level (see Figure 1). Also language use features seem to be central for the distinction of reading levels on both data sets. 30.4% of the features were selected for Spotlight-EN and 19.6% for Spotlight-DE. Four of the language use features are relevant for both data sets: the average word frequency and its standard deviation are decreasing with increasing reading level. The same holds for the log frequency of lexical word types. The standard deviation of the verb token frequency is increasing with higher reading levels. Lexical complexity seems to play a medium role in the distinction of reading levels. 13.5% of the lexical complexity features were selected for Spotlight-EN and 12.4% for Spotlight-DE. Especially lexical density and richness play an important role on both data sets, but there is only very little overlap between the features selected for Spotlight-EN and Spotlight-DE. Only the POS density of modifiers and proper nouns as well as the squared word TTR were selected on both feature sets. For English, the proper noun density is decreasing, while the POS density for modifiers and the squared word TTR are increasing with reading levels. For German, the squared word TTR is also increasing with reading levels, but the two POS density features exhibit a u-shaped and inverse u-shaped

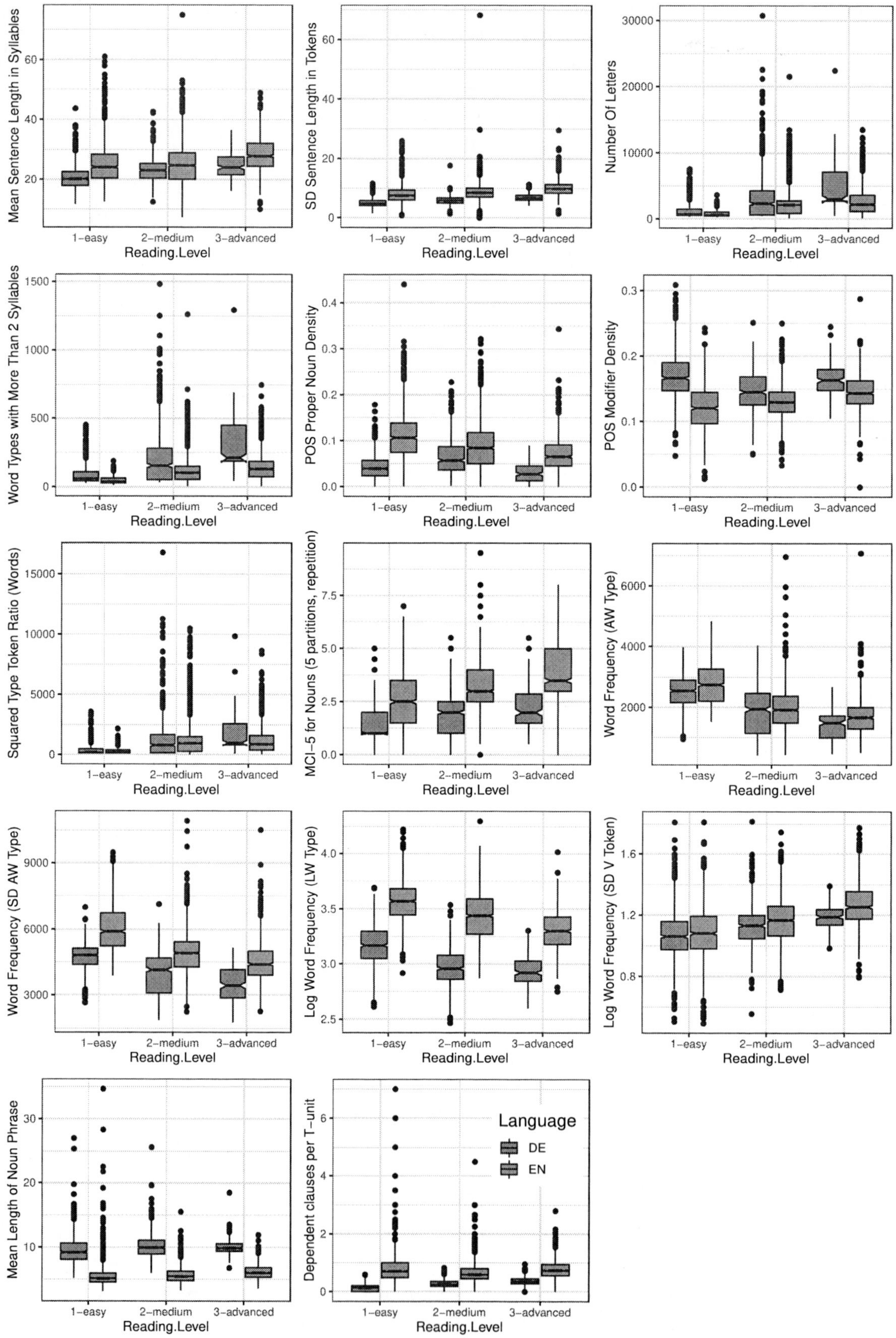

Figure 1: Boxplots of features that are informative on both, Spotlight-EN and Spotlight-DE

behavior.

The importance of syntactic and morphological complexity differs for Spotlight-EN and Spotlight-DE. Only 6.7% of the syntactic features were selected for Spotlight-EN, half of them features of syntactic variation. In contrast, 21.7% were selected on Spotlight-DE, all either features of clausal or phrasal complexity. Correspondingly, there is very little overlap in this domain between English an German. Only two syntactic features are informative for both data sets: the mean noun phrase length and the number of dependent clauses per t-unit, both of which are increasing with higher reading levels on both data sets. Morphological complexity features seem to play an important role for the distinction of reading levels on Spotlight-EN, but much less on Spotlight-DE. While 17.5% of the morphological complexity features were selected for Spotlight-EN, only 7.5% play a role on Spotight-DE. Both data sets share only one feature in this domain, namely the MCI for adjectives (measured with repetition with 5 partitions of size 5), which increases with higher reading levels, though the effect is more pronounced for English.

Neither implicit discourse cohesion features nor human language processing features seem to be important features on Spotlight-DE and also on Spotlight-EN, only 8.2% of the cohesion features were identified as informative.

7.3 Discussion

The correlation-based feature subset selection shows that features from most feature groups contribute meaningful information for the distinction of reading levels on both data sets. Especially features of surface length, language use, and lexical complexity help to characterize reading level differences on both data sets. Morphological and syntactic complexity features seem to capture more language-specific differences. There is also a considerable overlap of features selected for both data sets. Overall 28% of the features selected for Spotlight-EN and 32% of features selected for Spotlight-DE are shared between both data sets.

Judging from the features that are shared between the feature selections for English and German, higher reading levels are characterized by the use of less frequent vocabulary, longer words, sentences, and texts, and shifts in lexical density and richness. Also the features that were selected from the domains of morphological, phrasal and syntactic complexity increase with higher reading levels. This is in line with previous findings by Weiss and Meurers (2018) regarding the readability of German media texts targeting German-native speaking adults and children. However, our results indicate that these domains play a much less pronounced role for the distinction of reading levels. Interestingly, morphological elaboration seems to be more important for English than for German.

Human language processing measures do not seem to play an important role for the distinction of reading levels in either data sets, even though these measures are motivated by psycho-linguistic studies on human sentence processing. This is again in line with previous findings reported by Weiss and Meurers (2018).

Overall, these findings explain the albeit limited cross-language generalization of both readability classifiers in the zero-shot learning experiments. While there are differences in the types of features that are informative for the identification of reading levels across languages, there is nevertheless a substantial overlap and the shared features predominantly exhibit an increase in complexity with higher reading levels. This confirms that the publisher successfully instituted a policy facilitating the creation of stratified reading materials for different levels in a way that is comparable across the different languages that we analyzed.

8 Conclusion

We have investigated the use of language-independent broad linguistic complexity modeling for the multi-level readability classification of English and German reading materials for language learners. Our first study designed to benchmark the performance of our methods on the established OneStopEnglish yielded new state-of-the art results, clearly showcasing the value of broad linguistic modeling for readability assessment. Our study also shows that for certain tasks, broadly linguistically informed feature-based approaches are in fact not only competitive with neural approaches but exceeding their performance.

We then introduced a novel multi-level reading corpus for English and German on which we trained two readability classifiers that yield are highly successful within their respective training language. With this, we present the first multi-level readability classifier for German. This is highly relevant, because the much more commonly proposed binary classification approaches distinguishing simple and regular language are too limited to be of practical relevance for the retrieval of reading materials that are appropriate to foster foreign language learning.

We then demonstrated the generalizability of the German classifier for comparable English data and the English classifier for comparable German data. This is a novel contribution to cross-lingual readability research, not only because of the multi-level classification but also because of we propose a zero-shot cross-lingual readability classification approach unlike previous work focusing on augmenting low-resource training data. This is a central contribution to readability classification research, especially for languages other than English, given the lack of appropriate training materials for many languages.

In our final study, we compared the linguistic properties characterizing differences in reading levels in English and German. Our findings show that for both languages, texts systematically differ between reading levels in terms of the frequency and lexical complexity. Language-specific characteristics of reading levels can be found in the syntactic, discourse and morphological domains. The publisher thus successfully adapts the reading materials for different proficiency levels across a variety of linguistic domains in a systematic way. This is not a trivial insight, since previous work demonstrated that school book publishers do not always succeed in the linguistic adaptation of reading materials for different target groups (Berendes et al., 2018).

Our findings clearly demonstrate the value of feature-based classification approaches not only for the study of linguistic phenomena but also for readability classification. We demonstrate the feasibility of broad language-independent feature collections and their potential for zero-shot cross-lingual learning.

9 Outlook

As we saw in Table 7, cross-language zero-shot learning showed a promising result for training on Spotlight-DE and test on Spotlight-EN and the other way round. It is arguable that although different languages may complexify in different linguistic aspects, the general rule of more elaborate linguistic components and more varied expression usually resulting in higher complexity still applies. As a result, it is highly likely that zero-shot cross-language learning would also result in good performance, but detailed approaches need to be further designed and tested in future studies including more languages.

Another direction for future research is to see how the readability levels decided by the publisher match L2 learners' actual perception of the texts' difficulty. Although our models have yielded high accuracy, if the standards used to determine the levels of the texts do not actually match the learners' perceived difficulty, the predicted results are meaningless. Vajjala and Lučić (2019) offer an interesting data set that may potentially be used to answer this question.

Acknowledgements

We are grateful to the publisher Spotlight Verlag GmbH for making their publications available to us for research purposes.

References

Kepa Bengoetxea, Itziar González-Dios, and Amaia Aguirregoitia. 2020. AzterTest: Open source linguistic and stylistic analysis tool. *Procesamiento del Lenguaje Natural*, 64:61–68.

Rebekah George Benjamin. 2012. Reconstructing readability: Recent developments and recommendations in the analysis of text difficulty. *Educational Psychology Review*, 24:63–88.

Marc Benzahra and Yvon François. 2019. Measuring text readability with machine comprehension: a pilot study. In *Workshop on Building Educational Applications Using NLP*, pages 412–422.

Karin Berendes, Sowmya Vajjala, Detmar Meurers, Doreen Bryant, Wolfgang Wagner, Maria Chinkina, and Ulrich Trautwein. 2018. Reading demands in secondary school: Does the linguistic complexity of textbooks increase with grade level and the academic orientation of the school track? *Journal of Educational Psychology*, 110(4):518–543.

Bernd Bohnet and Joakim Nivre. 2012. A transition-based system for joint part-of-speech tagging and labeled non-projective dependency parsing. In *Proceedings of the 2012 Joint Conference on Empirical Methods in Natural Language Processing and Computational Natural Language Learning*, pages 1455–1465, Jeju Island, Korea. Association for Computational Linguistics.

Vaclav Brezina and Gabriele Pallotti. 2019. Morphological complexity in written L2 texts. *Second language research*, 35(1):99–119.

Tim Vor der Brück and Sven Hartrumpf. 2007. A semantically oriented readability checker for German. In *Proceedings of the 3rd Language & Technology Conference*, pages 270–274, Poznań, Poland. Wydawnictwo Poznańskie.

Marc Brysbaert, Matthias Buchmeier, Markus Conrad, Arthur M. Jacobs, Jens Bölte, and Andrea Böhl. 2011a. The word frequency effect: A review of recent developments and implications for the choice of frequency estimates in German. *Experimental Psychology*, 58:412–424.

Marc Brysbaert, Emmanuel Keuleers, and Boris New. 2011b. Assessing the usefulness of Google Books' word frequencies for psycholinguistic research on word processing. *Frontiers in Psychology*, 2(27).

Xiaobin Chen. 2018. *Automatic Analysis of Linguistic Complexity and Its Application in Language Learning Research.* Ph.D. thesis, Eberhard Karls Universität Tübingen Germany.

Xiaobin Chen and Detmar Meurers. 2017. Word frequency and readability: Predicting the text-level readability with a lexical-level attribute. *Journal of Research in Reading*, 41(3):486–510.

Xiaobin Chen and Detmar Meurers. 2018. Word frequency and readability: Predicting the text-level readability with a lexical-level attribute. *Journal of Research in Reading*, 41(3):486–510.

Xiaobin Chen and Detmar Meurers. 2019. Linking text readability and learner proficiency using linguistic complexity feature vector distance. *Computer-Assisted Language Learning*, 32(4):418–447. https://doi.org/10.1080/09588221.2018.1527358.

Maria Chinkina, Madeeswaran Kannan, and Detmar Meurers. 2016. Online information retrieval for language learning. In *Proceedings of ACL-2016 System Demonstrations*, pages 7–12, Berlin, Germany. Association for Computational Linguistics. http://anthology.aclweb.org/P16-4002.

Kevyn Collins-Thompson. 2014. Computational assessment of text readability: A survey of past, present, and future research. *International Journal of Applied Linguistics*, 165(2):97–135.

Scott A. Crossley. 2020. Linguistic features in writing quality and development: An overview. *Journal of Writing Research*, 11(3):415–443.

Scott A Crossley, Stephen Skalicky, Mihai Dascalu, Danielle S McNamara, and Kristopher Kyle. 2017. Predicting text comprehension, processing, and familiarity in adult readers: New approaches to readability formulas. *Discourse Processes*, 54(5-6):340–359.

Edgar Dale and Jeanne S. Chall. 1948. A formula for predicting readability. *Educational research bulletin; organ of the College of Education*, 27(1):11–28.

Orphée De Clercq and Véronique Hoste. 2016. All mixed up? Finding the optimal feature set for general readability prediction and its application to English and Dutch. *Computational Linguistics*, 42(3):457–490.

Felice Dell'Orletta, Simonetta Montemagni, and Giulia Venturi. 2013. Linguistic profiling of texts across textual genres and readability levels. An exploratory study on Italian fictional prose. In *Proceedings of Recent Advances in Natural Language Processing*.

Sabrina Dittrich, Zarah Weiss, Hannes Schröter, and Detmar Meurers. 2019. Integrating large-scale web data and curated corpus data in a search engine supporting German literacy education. In *Proceedings of the 8th Workshop on NLP for Computer Assisted Language Learning*, pages 41–56, Turku, Finland.

William H. DuBay. 2006. *The Classic Readability Studies*. Impact Information, Costa Mesa, California.

Nick Ellis and Laura Collins. 2009. Input and second language acquisition: The roles of frequency, form, and function. Introduction to the special issue. *The Modern Language Journal*, 93(3):329–335.

B. Janghorban Esfahani, A. Faron, K. S. Roth, P. P. Grimminger, and J. C. Luers. 2016. Systematic readability analysis of medical texts on websites of German university clinics for general and abdominal surgery. *Zentralblatt fur Chirurgie*, 141(6):639–644.

Rudolf Franz Flesch. 1948. A new readability yardstick. *Journal of Applied Psychology*, 32(3):221–233.

Thomas François and Cedrick Fairon. 2012. An "AI readability" formula for French as a foreign language. In *Proceedings of the 2012 Joint Conference on Empirical Methods in Natural Language Processing and Computational Natural Language Learning*. https://www.aclweb.org/anthology/D12-1043.

Edward Gibson. 2000. The dependency locality theory: A distance-based theory of linguistic complexity. In Alec Marantz, Yasushi Miyashita, and Wayne O'Neil, editors, *Image, language, brain: papers from the First Mind Articulation Project Symposium*, pages 95–126. MIT.

Itziar Gonzalez-Dios, María Jesús Aranzabe, Arantza Díaz de Ilarraza, and Haritz Salaberri. 2014. Simple or complex? Assessing the readability of Basque texts. In *Proceedings of COLING 2014, the 25th International Conference on Computational Linguistics: Technical Papers*, pages 334–344, Dublin, Ireland. Dublin City University and Association for Computational Linguistics.

Petronella Grootens-Wiegers, Martine C. De Vries, Tessa E. Vossen, and Jos M. Van den Broek. 2015.

Readability and visuals in medical research information forms for children and adolescents. *Science Communication*, 37(1):89–117.

Mark Hall, Eibe Frank, Geoffrey Holmes, Bernhard Pfahringer, Peter Reutemann, and Ian H. Witten. 2009. The WEKA data mining software: An update. In *The SIGKDD Explorations*, volume 11, pages 10–18.

Mark A Hall. 1999. *Correlation-based feature selection for machine learning*. Ph.D. thesis, The University of Waikato.

Julia Hancke, Sowmya Vajjala, and Detmar Meurers. 2012. Readability classification for German using lexical, syntactic, and morphological features. In *Proceedings of the 24th International Conference on Computational Linguistics (COLING)*, pages 1063–1080, Mumbai, India. http://aclweb.org/anthology-new/C/C12/C12-1065.pdf.

Stephen D. Krashen. 1981. The fundamental pedagogical principle in second language teaching. *Studia Linguistica*, 35(1–2):50–70.

Christoph Kühberger, Christoph Bramann, Zarah Weiss, and Detmar Meurers. 2019. Task complexity in history textbooks. a multidisciplinary case study on triangulation in history education research. *History Education International Research Journal (HEIRJ)*, 16(1). Special Issue on Mixed Methods and Triangulation in History Education Research.

Max Kuhn. 2020. caret: Classification and regression training. R package version 6.0-86.

Kristopher Kyle. 2016. *Measuring Syntactic Development in L2 Writing: Fine Grained Indices of Syntactic Complexity and Usage-Based Indices of Syntactic Sophistication*. Ph.D. thesis, Georgia State University.

James P Lantolf, Stephen L Thorne, and Matthew E Poehner. 2015. Sociocultural theory and second language development. In *Theories in second language acquisition: An introduction*. Routledge New York, NY.

Roger Levy and Galen Andrew. 2006. Tregex and Tsurgeon: tools for querying and manipulating tree data structures. In *5th International Conference on Language Resources and Evaluation*, Genoa, Italy.

Ion Madrazo Azpiazu and Maria Soledad Pera. 2019. Multiattentive recurrent neural network architecture for multilingual readability assessment. *Transactions of the Association for Computational Linguistics*, 7:421–436.

Ion Madrazo Azpiazu and Maria Soledad Pera. 2020a. An analysis of transfer learning methods for multilingual readability assessment. *Adjunct Publication of the 28th ACM Conference on User Modeling, Adaptation and Personalization*, pages 95–100.

Ion Madrazo Azpiazu and Maria Soledad Pera. 2020b. Is cross-lingual readability assessment possible? *Journal of the Association for Information Science and Technology*.

Christopher D. Manning, Mihai Surdeanu, John Bauer, Jenny Finkel, Steven J. Bethard, and David McClosky. 2014. The Stanford CoreNLP natural language processing toolkit. In *Association for Computational Linguistics (ACL) System Demonstrations*, pages 55–60. http://aclweb.org/anthology/P/P14/P14-5010.

Matej Martinc, Senja Pollak, and Marko Robnik-Šikonja. 2019. Supervised and unsupervised neural approaches to text readability. *arXiv preprint arXiv:1907.11779*.

Philip M. McCarthy and Scott Jarvis. 2007. A theoretical and empirical evaluation of vocd. *Language Testing*, 24:459–488.

Danielle A. McNamara, Arthur C. Graesser, Philip M. McCarthy, and Zhiqiang Cai. 2014. *Automated evaluation of text and discourse with Coh-Metrix*. Cambridge University Press, Cambridge, M.A.

Eleni Miltsakaki and Audrey Troutt. 2007. Read-x: Automatic evaluation of reading difficulty of web text. In *Proceedings of World Conference on E-Learning in Corporate, Government, Healthcare, and Higher Education 2007*, pages 7280–7286, Quebec City, Canada. AACE. http://www.editlib.org/p/26932.

Ildikó Pilán, Sowmya Vajjala, and Elena Volodina. 2015. A readable read: Automatic assessment of language learning materials based on linguistic complexity. In *Proceedings of CICLING 2015- Research in Computing Science Journal Issue (to appear)*. https://arxiv.org/abs/1603.08868.

R Core Team. 2015. *R: A Language and Environment for Statistical Computing*. R Foundation for Statistical Computing, Vienna, Austria.

Robert Reynolds. 2016. *Russian natural language processing for computer-assisted language learning: capturing the benefits of deep morphological analysis in real-life applications*. Ph.D. thesis, UiT - The Arctic University of Norway.

Cory Shain, Marten van Schijndel, Richard Futrell, Edward Gibson, and William Schuler. 2016. Memory access during incremental sentence processing causes reading time latency. In *Proceedings of the Workshop on Computational Linguistics for Linguistic Complexity (CL4LC)*, pages 49–58, Osaka.

Emma Strubell, Ananya Ganesh, and Andrew McCallum. 2019. Energy and policy considerations for deep learning in NLP. In *Proceedings of the 57th Annual Meeting of the Association for Computational Linguistics*, pages 3645–3650, Florence, Italy. Association for Computational Linguistics.

Sowmya Vajjala and Ivana Lučić. 2018. OneStopEnglish corpus: A new corpus for automatic readability assessment and text simplification. In *Proceedings of the thirteenth workshop on innovative use of NLP for building educational applications*, pages 297–304.

Sowmya Vajjala and Ivana Lučić. 2019. On understanding the relation between expert annotations of text readability and target reader comprehension. In *Proceedings of the Fourteenth Workshop on Innovative Use of NLP for Building Educational Applications*, pages 349–359.

Sowmya Vajjala and Detmar Meurers. 2012. On improving the accuracy of readability classification using insights from second language acquisition. In *Proceedings of the Seventh Workshop on Building Educational Applications Using NLP*, pages 163–173. http://aclweb.org/anthology/W12-2019.pdf.

Zarah Weiss, Sabrina Dittrich, and Detmar Meurers. 2018. A linguistically-informed search engine to identifiy reading material for functional illiteracy classes. In *Proceedings of the 7th Workshop on Natural Language Processing for Computer-Assisted Language Learning (NLP4CALL)*.

Zarah Weiss and Detmar Meurers. 2018. Modeling the readability of German targeting adults and children: An empirically broad analysis and its cross-corpus validation. In *Proceedings of the 27th International Conference on Computational Linguistics (COLING)*, Santa Fe, New Mexico, USA. https://www.aclweb.org/anthology/C18-1026.

Zarah Weiss and Detmar Meurers. 2019a. Analyzing linguistic complexity and accuracy in academic language development of German across elementary and secondary school. In *Proceedings of the 14th Workshop on Innovative Use of NLP for Building Educational Applications (BEA)*, Florence, Italy. Association for Computational Linguistics.

Zarah Weiss and Detmar Meurers. 2019b. Broad linguistic modeling is beneficial for German L2 proficiency assessment. In *Widening the Scope of Learner Corpus Research. Selected Papers from the Fourth Learner Corpus Research Conference*, Louvain-La-Neuve. Presses Universitaires de Louvain.

Zarah Weiss and Detmar Meurers. 2021. Analyzing the linguistic complexity of German learner language in a reading comprehension task: Using proficiency classification to investigate short answer data, cross-data generalizability, and the impact of linguistic analysis quality. *International Journal of Learner Corpus Research*, 7(1):84–131.

Zarah Weiss, Anja Riemenschneider, Pauline Schröter, and Detmar Meurers. 2019. Computationally modeling the impact of task-appropriate language complexity and accuracy on human grading of German essays. In *Proceedings of the 14th Workshop on Innovative Use of NLP for Building Educational Applications (BEA)*, Florence, Italy.

Kate Wolfe-Quintero, Shunji Inagaki, and Hae-Young Kim. 1998. *Second Language Development in Writing: Measures of Fluency, Accuracy & Complexity*. Second Language Teaching & Curriculum Center, University of Hawaii at Manoa, Honolulu.

Victoria Yaneva, Irina Temnikova, and Ruslan Mitkov. 2016. Accessible texts for autism: An eye-tracking study. In *Proceedings of the 17th International ACM SIGACCESS Conference on Computers & Accessibility*, pages 49–57.

Appendix A: List of Selected Features

A.1: Features selected for Spotlight-EN

LEN Number Of Letters, SD Token Length in Letters, Percentage of Word Types with More Than 2 Syllables Length Measures, Number of Word Types with More Than 2 Syllables, SD Sentence Length in Tokens, SD Sentence Length in Syllables, Mean Sentence Length in Syllables

SYN Syntactic Complexity Feature: Dependent clauses per T-unit Clausal, Syntactic Complexity Feature: Mean Length of Noun Phrase Phrasal, SD Local Edit Distance for tokens, SD Global Edit Distance for Lemmas

LEX POS Density Feature: Particle, POS Density Feature: Adjective, POS Density Feature: Past Participle Verb, POS Density Feature: Article, POS Density Feature: Coordinating Conjunction, POS Density Feature: Modifier, POS Proper Noun Density, Corrected TTR, Corrected TTR Adjectives, Suqared TTR Words, Uber index (10) Adjectives, Lexical Verb Variation

MOR MCI-5 for Verbs (5 partitions no repetition), MCI-5 for Nouns (5 partitions no repetition), MCI-10 for Nouns (5 partitions no repetition), MCI-5 for Adjectives (2 partitions with repetition), MCI-5 for Adjectives (2 partitions no repetition), MCI-5 for Nouns (5 partitions with repetition), MCI-5 for Nouns (10 partitions no repetition)

DIS Global Lemma Overlap, Mean Local Noun Overlap (word form-based)

USE Logarithmic Word Frequency (Adj Type), Logarithmic Word Frequency (FW Type),

Logarithmic Word Frequency (SD Adj Token), Logarithmic Word Frequency (SD FW Type), Logarithmic Word Frequency (LW Type), Logarithmic Word Frequency (SD V Type), Logarithmic Word Frequency (AW Type), Word Frequency (AW Type), Logarithmic Word Frequency (V Type), Word Frequency (SD AW Token), Logarithmic Word Frequency (SD LW Token), Word Frequency (FW Token), Logarithmic Word Frequency (SD V Token), Logarithmic Word Frequency (Adv Token), Word Frequency (SD AW Type), Logarithmic Word Frequency (SD LW Type), Word Frequency (SD FW Type)

HLP *none*

A.2: Features selected for Spotlight-DE

LEN Number Of Letters, 2 Number of Word Types with More Than 2 Syllables, Mean Sentence Length in Syllables, SD Sentence Length in Tokens, SD Sentence Length in Letters

SYN Relative Clauses per Sentence, Relative Clauses per Clause, Dependent clauses per Sentence, Dependent clauses per T-unit, Complex T-unit Ratio, Dependent clause ratio, Relative Clauses per T-Unit, Mean Length of T-unit, Verb Cluster per T-Unit, Mean Length of Noun Phrase, Postnominal Modifier per Complex Noun Phrase, Verb Phrases per Clause, Verb Phrases per T-unit

LEX TTR Adverbs per Lexical Types, Squared TTR Nouns, Uber index (10) Verbs, Uber index (10) Nouns, Squared TTR Words, Modals per Verb, POS Modifier Density, POS To-infinitive Density, POS Possessive Pronoun Density, POS Proper Noun Density

MOR MCI-5 for Nouns (2 partitions with repetition), MCI-5 for Nouns (5 partitions with repetition), MCI-10 for Nouns (2 partitions no repetition)

DIS *none*

USE Word Frequency (V Type), Word Frequency (SD V Type), Logarithmic Word Frequency (Adj Token), Logarithmic Word Frequency (SD V Token), Word Frequency (AW Type), Logarithmic Word Frequency (SD Adv Token), Logarithmic Word Frequency (LW Type), Logarithmic Word Frequency (V Token), Word Frequency (SD FW Token), Logarithmic Word Frequency (SD AW Token), Word Frequency (SD AW Type)

HLP *none*

Developing Flashcards for Learning Icelandic

Xindan Xu
University of Iceland
Reykjavík, Iceland
xindanxu@hi.is

Anton Karl Ingason
University of Iceland
Reykjavík, Iceland
antoni@hi.is

Abstract

This paper describes the process of developing flashcards for the most frequently used words in Icelandic. The process involves utilising currently available open-source online databases, the Tagged Icelandic Corpus, MÍM, and the Database of Modern Icelandic Inflection, BÍN, to extract a list of the most frequently used words, their part-of-speech tags, and inflectional forms. This was combined with newly developed language technology tools for Icelandic to generate phonetic and audio transcriptions of the words. The final product is a combination of printable flashcards and digital flashcards which are easily accessible through smart devices.

1 Introduction

Flashcards are a useful tool for learning. They are frequently used for memorising new words when learning a new language. When combined with spaced repetition, they can produce long-term knowledge retention.

In this project, we created a deck of flashcards that consists of the 4,000 most frequently used words in Icelandic. On the front side of each flashcard, a word is shown along with a sample sentence. On the back of each flashcard, more detailed information about the word is shown, including the following: its English translation, essential morpho-syntactic information (e.g. word class and gender, if applicable), the phonetic transcription, dialectal variation (if applicable), and selected inflectional forms.

The production of this flashcard dataset was made possible due to the recent developments in language technologies for Icelandic. Twenty years ago, this project would have to be carried out manually because Icelandic language technology resources were almost non-existent (Rögnvaldsson et al., 2009). Since 2000, a lot of effort and financial support have been put into developing language technologies for Icelandic. This included building online corpora of texts and sound files, e.g. the Tagged Icelandic Corpus MÍM (Helgadóttir et al., 2012), online dictionaries, e.g. The Database of Modern Icelandic Inflection BÍN (Bjarnadóttir, 2012), and basic tools for natural language processing, e.g. IceTagger (Loftsson, 2008) and Lemmald (Ingason et al., 2008).

By utilising these resources, we have compiled a novel dataset that contains a rich variety of information for selected words. This information was incorporated into flashcards to create a more detailed and effective learning material. We developed two versions of the flashcards: a printable pdf-version and a digital Anki-version that supports media files and is available on multiple platforms. Both versions of the flashcards will be accessible to the public without charge, and the dataset will be published under an open-source license (CC BY 4.0).

2 Flashcards for vocabulary learning

Vocabulary learning is a fundamental aspect of second language acquisition and lasts throughout the learning process. Vocabulary learning involves two scopes: vocabulary size and depth of vocabulary knowledge (Schmitt, 2008). Without sufficient vocabulary size, understanding input and producing satisfactory output in a second language can be frustrating for learners. Furthermore, a lexical item is learned not only by making a form-

Xindan Xu and Anton Karl Ingason 2021. Developing flashcards for learning Icelandic. *Proceedings of the 10th Workshop on Natural Language Processing for Computer Assisted Language Learning (NLP4CALL 2021)*. Linköping Electronic Conference Proceedings 177: 55–61.

meaning connection, but also by understanding how it is used in context (Schmitt, 2008).

Flashcards are a learning tool that facilitates the acquisition of vocabulary. Through the use of high frequency words of a second language, flashcards can help acquire sufficient vocabulary size more effectively. Flashcards can also provide lexical items with context, as well as additional information that aids the depth of vocabulary knowledge, for example, word class, pronunciation and inflectional forms. Furthermore, flashcards can incorporate spaced repetition learning that can produce long-term knowledge retention of the vocabulary. Studies have shown that spaced repetition is one of the most effective learning techniques (Dunlosky et al., 2013; Kang, 2016). This is a learning technique that allows initial study and subsequent reviews to be spaced out over time, and that new and more difficult material is reviewed more often than well-known and easy material.

3 Source of material

Vocabulary and associated morphological information was extracted from two main sources: the Tagged Icelandic Corpus, MÍM (Helgadóttir et al., 2012), and the Database of Mordern Icelandic Inflection, BÍN (Bjarnadóttir, 2012).

3.1 MÍM corpus

The Tagged Icelandic Corpus (hereafter referred to as MÍM) contains approximately 25 million tokens collected from contemporary Icelandic texts during the period 2006–2010. The texts are selected from a variety of sources, including published books, newspapers, Icelandic parliament speeches, legal texts, and student essays. These texts are considered to be representative of the Icelandic society's language usage. The texts are morphosyntactically tagged, lemmatized, and formatted into XML-documents defined by TEI (Text Encoding Initiative). This makes it possible to extract a variety of useful information from the corpus. In this study, we extracted the frequency of headwords and their part-of-speech tags, as well as sample sentences for the selected headwords.

The corpus was tagged and lemmatized automatically using software *IceNLP* (Loftsson, 2019). The accuracy of morphosyntactic tagging was estimated to be 88.1%–95.1% depending on text type (Loftsson et al., 2010). The accuracy of lemmatization was estimated to be approximately 90%. The corpus is available through a special user license.[1]

An example of entries for the headword *ár* (e. *year*) in the MÍM corpus is shown in Listing 1. The inflectional form of the headword is shown between <w> and </w>: *árum* and *ára*. Type shows the POS-tag used for the inflectional form, i.e. "nhfþ" for *árum* and "nhfe" for *ára*.[2]

```
<w lemma="ár" type="nhfþ">árum</w>
<w lemma="ár" type="nhfe">ára</w>
```

Listing 1: Example from the MÍM Corpus

The first character in the tag always shows the word class, e.g. "n" for "nafnorð" (e. *noun*), "s" for "sagnorð" (e. *verb*). The number of characters used in the tag depends on the word class. In this case, "árum" in the first entry was tagged: noun, neutral, plural and dative, whilst "ára" in the second entry was tagged: noun, neutral, plural and genitive.

3.2 BÍN corpus

The Database of Modern Icelandic Inflection (hereafter referred to as BÍN) consists of more than 270,000 headwords with approximately 5.8 million inflectional forms. Language technology data from the database are distributed under a CC BY-SA 4.0 license and are available at `https://bin.arnastofnun.is/DMII/`. The basic version of the database, Sigrún's format, was used in the development of the flashcards. The data consists of 6 fields: lemma, id, word class, semantic fields, inflectional form, and grammatical tag (see example of *ár* in Figure 1).

4 Data processing

A Python script was used to parse XML-documents and count the frequency of occurrence for each pair of lemma and the first two characters of the tag in the MÍM corpus. The resulting dataset was cleaned and expanded upon by comparison with the BÍN corpus.

Unnecessary tokens in the resulting dataset (e.g. symbols and roman numbers) were filtered out by comparing all the entries with the headword entries in the BÍN corpus. Subsequently, since the MÍM corpus was tagged and lemmatized automatically, it was necessary to double-check the extracted tags

[1] See `http://www.malfong.is/files/userlicense_mim_download_en.pdf`.

[2] See the full list of tagsets used in MÍM corpus: `http://www.malfong.is/files/mim_tagset_files_en.pdf`.

```
     lemma  ind cat   bin_tag word_form tag
     <chr> <dbl> <chr> <chr>  <chr>     <chr>
   1 ár      466 hk    alm    ár        NFET
   2 ár      466 hk    alm    árið      NFETgr
   3 ár      466 hk    alm    ár        ÞFET
   4 ár      466 hk    alm    árið      ÞFETgr
   5 ár      466 hk    alm    ári       ÞGFET
   6 ár      466 hk    alm    árinu     ÞGFETgr
   7 ár      466 hk    alm    árs       EFET
   8 ár      466 hk    alm    ársins    EFETgr
   9 ár      466 hk    alm    ár        NFFT
  10 ár      466 hk    alm    árin      NFFTgr
  11 ár      466 hk    alm    ár        ÞFFT
  12 ár      466 hk    alm    árin      ÞFFTgr
  13 ár      466 hk    alm    árum      ÞGFFT
  14 ár      466 hk    alm    árunum    ÞGFFTgr
  15 ár      466 hk    alm    ára       EFFT
  16 ár      466 hk    alm    áranna    EFFTgr
```

Figure 1: Example of the entry for *ár* in the BÍN corpus.

and make corrections where necessary. For example, prepositions and adverbs share the same tag ("a") in the MÍM corpus, whilst they have separate tags in the BÍN corpus ("fs" for prepositions and "ao" for adverbs). Furthermore, a lemma can be two or more separate words from different word classes. For example, lemma *sig* can be both a neutral noun meaning "subsidence", and a reflexive pronoun referring to oneself. To make sure these instances are tagged correctly, all the headwords and tags extracted from the MÍM corpus were compared against tags in the BÍN corpus. If the tags did not match, the tags from the BÍN corpus were used. Finally, words were ranked by their frequency of occurrence and the top 4,000 were chosen for the project.

As it would not be beneficial to show all the inflectional forms of a headword at once, selected inflectional forms were chosen based on word class. Selected inflectional forms of the chosen words were retrieved from the BÍN corpus. An example entry for the noun *ár* is shown in the Table 1. In this case, the frequency of occurrence of lemma "ár" of class "hk" in the MÍM corpus was 96,849 times. This was ranked 29th amongst all the headwords in the MÍM corpus. Its genitive singular form (EFET) is *árs* and nominative plural form (NFFT) is *ár*.

Lemma	Class	Freq	Rank	W_form	Tag
ár	hk	96,849	29	árs ár	EFET NFFT

Table 1: Example entry for the noun *ár*.

4.1 Phonetic and audio transcription

Phonetic transcriptions of the words were generated using LSTM encoder-decoder sequence-to-sequence models developed by Grammatek ehf. (2021). These models transcribe grapheme to phoneme (g2p) in four pronunciation variants of Icelandic: the standard pronunciation of modern Icelandic, the northern variant (post-aspiration), the southern variant (hv-pronunciation), and the northeast variant (post-aspiration + voiced pronunciation).[3] The R package ipa (Hayes and Alexander, 2020) was used to convert the X-SAMPA phonetic transcription resulting from the g2p models to ipa transcription.

In Icelandic, the pronunciation of a lemma is the same in different word classes. For example, the lemma *tala* can be used as a feminine noun meaning "number, speech", or as a verb meaning "talk, speak". In both instances, pronunciation of the lemma is the same: [tʰaːla]. Accounting for these duplicates, a total of 3,933 unique lemmas (out of 4,000 in total) was used for phonetic transcription.

Audio transcriptions were generated using the Icelandic Dóra voice included in the Amazon Polly text-to-speech service (Amazon Web Services, 2021).

4.2 Translation and sample sentence

Translation of the Icelandic words was carried out semi-automatically. A list of words was translated automatically using the Google Translate web service. However, the translation accuracy turned out to be poor in some cases. Poor translation accuracy mainly occurs when there is minimal difference in written form between two different words. For example, lemma *hár* can be a noun meaning "hair" and an adjective meaning "high". In such cases, Google Translate failed to differentiate the word class and their meanings. Furthermore, Google Translate did not recognise the acute accent in some cases. For example, *dýr* (e. *animal* (no.) and *expensive* (adj.)) and *dyr* (e. *door*) are only distinguished by the acute accent, but they were both translated into "animals" using Google Translate. According to a recent study (Aiken, 2019), Icelandic was among the lowest scoring languages in terms of translation accuracy using Google translate. Therefore, translations were reviewed manually using the Concise Icelandic-English Dictio-

[3]For more information about the regional pronunciation variants of Icelandic, see Rögnvaldsson (2020).

nary (Hólmarsson et al., 2006) as a reference.

The process of selecting sample sentences was also carried out semi-automatically. A python script was used to parse the XML-files from the MÍM corpus and 10 sentences were selected for each headword. Subsequently, sentences were arranged based on their complexity, i.e., length of the sentence and whether there are any uncommon words in the sentence. Finally, the most easily understandable sentence was selected manually for each headword to be shown on the flashcards.

After this step, the data was ready to be used in the production of the flashcards. Table 2 shows a demonstration data-frame with all information excluding the sample sentences and selected inflectional forms.

4.3 Printable and digital flashcards

Both a printable pdf version and a digital version of the flashcards were made in the project. The pdf version of the flashcards was generated using the R package Knitr (Xie, 2021) and the LaTeX-package Flacards (Stuhrmann, 2005). The main difference between the two versions is that the digital version contains audio files of the selected words so that users can listen to their pronunciation; while the physical flashcards contain the phonetic transcriptions in regional variants of Icelandic (if applicable).

Digital flashcards

Digital flashcards were made using the Python library Genanki (Staley, 2021). The script produces an Anki-deck package which can be imported into the Anki-app. Anki is available on multiple platforms and supports different media types in the cards. Another advantage of Anki is the inclusion of spaced repetition, which is considered to be one of the most effective learning techniques (Dunlosky et al., 2013; Kang, 2016).

Basic components of an Anki deck are notes. Each note contains a front (question) and a back (answer) side with information to memorise. The notes in the Genanki library are defined by two components:

1. *models*, which indicate the information to be shown on the card by defining the *fields* and how the card should look like by defining the *templates*.

2. *fields*, which are the actual information to be shown on the card and should correspond to the fields defined by the model.

The difference between the *fields* in the model and the *fields* in the note is that the fields in the model act like a placeholder for the fields of information to be shown, while the fields in the notes are the actual information.

Figure 2 shows an example of the front and back of the Anki flashcard for *ár*. The triangle button which is located next to the phonetic transcription is used to replay the audio of the word. At the bottom of the user interface, the user can choose the interval between repeated viewings. A short interval should be chosen for flashcards that are difficult to memorise so that they are repeated more frequently, whilst a long interval should be chosen for flashcards that are easy to memorise. This process is done to prioritise the flashcards that are harder to learn and thus to improve the overall efficiency of learning. For example, the card would be reviewed immediately by clicking the "again" button, after 1 day by clicking the "Good" button, and after 4 days by clicking "Easy" button. Different interval settings can be selected by the user on their Anki app.

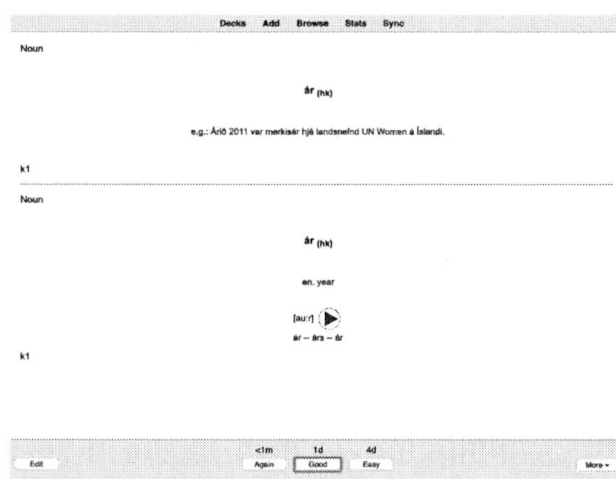

Figure 2: Example of the front and back of the flashcard for *ár* in Anki.

Printable flashcards

Despite all the advantages that Anki offers, some studies also showed that physical flashcards may produce learning outcomes similar to those for digital flashcards (Sage et al., 2020; Nikoopour and Kazemi, 2014). Furthermore, studies have shown that digital flashcards on mobile devices have led to distractions (Sage et al., 2020) and low enjoyment (Hanson and Brown, 2019) amongst students.

lemma	cat	freq	rank	ipa_sd	ipa_north	ipa_northeast	ipa_south	full_cat	eng
vera	so	1,083,582	1	vɛːra	vɛːra	vɛːra	vɛːra	Verb	be
og	st	953,690	2	ɔːɣ	ɔɣ	ɔɣ	ɔɣ	Conjunction	and
í	fs	810,646	3	iː	iː	iː	iː	Preposition	to; in
að	nhm	540,429	5	aːð	aːð	aːð	aːð	Infinitive marker	to
það	pfn	495,273	6	θaːð	θað	θaːð	θaːð	Pronoun	it, that
ekki	ao	209,020	16	ɛhcɪ	ɛhcɪ	ɛhcɪ	ɛhcɪ	Adverb	not
ár	hk	96,849	29	auːr	auːr	auːr	auːr	Noun	year
mikill	lo	75,043	42	mɪːcɪtl̥	mɪːcʰɪtl̥	mɪːcʰɪtl̥	mɪːcʰɪtl̥	Adjective	large, big; much; great
einn	to	50,885	54	eitn̥	eitn̥	eitn̥	eitn̥	Numeral	one
hinn	gr	27,844	94	hɪn	hɪn	hɪn	hɪn	Article	that, the other
nei	uh	6,774	345	nei:	nei:	nei:	nei:	Interjection	no

Table 2: A demonstration data-frame for flashcard production.

The pdf-version of the flashcards is generated by a mother RNW document and eight child RNW documents. The mother RNW document defines the document class *flacards*, reads in the dataset (similar to the one shown in Table 2), and loops through each row to create the respective flashcard. The child RNW documents define different presentations of the cards for different word classes. For example, three inflectional forms were chosen for the word classes *noun* (lemma, genitive singular and nominative plural), *personal pronoun* (lemma, genitive singular and nominative plural), and *verb* (3rd person singular in present tense and past tense, and past participle in neuter singular nominative case). Four child RNW documents were created to accommodate different word classes. Subsequently, four corresponding child RNW documents were created to accommodate the regional pronunciation variants. For each row in the dataset, the mother RNW document selected the child RNW document required to produce the flashcard. For example, the child RNW document for the word class *noun* without pronunciation variant would be selected for the noun *ár*, whilst the child RNW document for adjective with pronunciation variant would be selected for the adjective *mikill* (Figure 3).[4]

The front side of the pdf-version (Figure 3) is the same as the Anki version (Figure 2). On the back side of the pdf-version, regional variants of pronunciation are shown (Figure 3) as opposed to the audio version of the word in the Anki-version (Figure 2). The noun *ár* has the same pronunciation across all regions of Iceland. The adjective *mikill* has regional pronunciation variants in the north and northeast regions of Iceland (Figure 3).

[4]The abbreviations *fst*, *mst* and *est* in Figure 3 refer to *positive degree*, *comparative degree* and *superlative degree* respectively.

Figure 3: Example of the front and back side of the pdf flashcard for *ár* and *mikill*.

5 Summary and future implementations

In this paper, we have described the process of the production of printable and digital flashcards for the most frequently used words in Icelandic (based on the MÍM corpus). The flashcards dataset will be published under an open-source license which means that it will be freely accessible to the public for use and as a template for further flashcard production.

The flashcards will be useful for anyone who is interested in learning Icelandic, especially at the beginning stage where large quantities of vocabulary need to be acquired. By learning the high frequency words in the language, learners can understand a high percentage of words in common texts such as newspapers and books.

During the production of the flashcards, all steps were carried out automatically except for translation and selecting sample sentences which were both semi-automatic (Table 3). The most time consuming parts are, as expected, the manual steps:

double-checking the translation accuracy and selecting sample sentences.

	Steps	Efficiency
1	Extract word lists and frequency from MÍM	Automatic
2	Filter out undesirable entries by comparing against lemmas in BÍN corpus	Automatic
3	Extract selected inflectional forms from BÍN	Automatic
4	Phonetic transcription	Automatic
5	Audio transcription	Automatic
6	Translation	Semi-automatic
7	Sample sentences	Semi-automatic
8	Generate printable flashcards	Automatic
9	Generate Anki-flashcards	Automatic

Table 3: Summary steps for the production of flashcards in the project.

A complete list of resources used for the development of the flashcards and their respective licenses are shown in Table 4.

Resource	License
MÍM	Special User License
BÍN	CC BY-SA 4.0 license
g2p-lstm	Apache License 2.0
ipa	MIT | Alexander Rossell Hayes (2020)
Amazon Polly	Creative Commons Attribution-ShareAlike 4.0 International Public License
Genanki	MIT
Knitr	GPL-2 | GPL-3
Flacards	GNU General Public License

Table 4: List of resources used and information about their licences.

In conclusion, we have described the development of a flashcard dataset for leaning Icelandic. The work will serve as a useful template for further development of flashcards as a learning material for Icelandic. For example, a variety of practice decks of the Anki-version can be made so that users can test their learning progress. In Anki, a cloze-deletion field or type-in text field can be implemented into the front of a card. The user's answer will be reviewed automatically and shown in the back (answer) side of the flashcard. This could easily be incorporated into the flashcards so that users can type in the Icelandic words according to the English translation or the phonetic transcription of words with audio display.

Furthermore, the two flashcard decks will serve as a useful resource for the evaluation of flashcards as a learning material, and to ascertain the relative benefits of digital versus physical flashcards for second language learners. We leave that for future work.

Acknowledgements

We would like to thank Anna Björk Nikulásdóttir for the phonetic transcription models, and Atli Jasonarson for writing a script that submitted our word list to Amazon Polly to generate the sound files.

References

Milam Aiken. 2019. An updated evaluation of google translate accuracy. *Studies in Linguistics and Literature*, 3:p253.

Amazon Web Services. 2021. Amazon Polly. `https://aws.amazon.com/polly/`.

Kristín Bjarnadóttir. 2012. The Database of Modern Icelandic Inflection (Beygingarlýsing íslensks nútímamáls). In *LREC 2012 Proceedings: Proceedings of "Language Technology for Normalisation of Less-Resourced Languages"*, pages 13–18.

John Dunlosky, Katherine A. Rawson, Elizabeth J. Marsh, Mitchell J. Nathan, and Daniel T. Willingham. 2013. Improving students' learning with effective learning techniques: Promising directions from cognitive and educational psychology. *Psychological Science in the Public Interest*, 14(1):4–58. PMID: 26173288.

Grammatek ehf. 2021. g2p-lstm. Phonetic transcription tool. `https://github.com/grammatek/g2p-lstm.git`.

Aroline Hanson and Christina Brown. 2019. Enhancing l2 learning through a mobile assisted spaced-repetition tool: an effective but bitter pill? *Computer Assisted Language Learning*, 33:1–23.

Rossell Hayes and Alexander. 2020. *ipa: convert between phonetic alphabets*. R package version 0.1.0.

Sigrún Helgadóttir, Ásta Svavarsdóttir, Eiríkur Rögnvaldsson, Kristín Bjarnadóttir, and Hrafn Loftsson. 2012. The Tagged Icelandic Corpus (MÍM). In *Proceedings of the Workshop on Language Technology for Normalisation of Less-Resourced Languages*, pages 67–72.

Sverrir Hólmarsson, Christopher Sanders, and John Tucker. 2006. Íslensk-ensk orðabók / Concise Icelandic-English Dictionary.

Anton Karl Ingason, Sigrún Helgadóttir, Hrafn Loftsson, and Eiríkur Rögnvaldsson. 2008. A mixed method lemmatization algorithm using a hierarchy of linguistic identities (holi). In *Advances in Natural Language Processing*, pages 205–216, Berlin, Heidelberg. Springer Berlin Heidelberg.

Sean H. K. Kang. 2016. Spaced repetition promotes efficient and effective learning: Policy implications for instruction. *Policy Insights from the Behavioral and Brain Sciences*, 3(1):12–19.

Hrafn Loftsson. 2008. Tagging icelandic text: A linguistic rule-based approach. *Nordic Journal of Linguistics*, 31(1):47–72.

Hrafn Loftsson. 2019. IceNLP natural language processing toolkit. CLARIN-IS, Stofnun Árna Magnússonar.

Hrafn Loftsson, Jökull H. Yngvason, Sigrún Helgadóttir, and Eiríkur Rögnvaldsson. 2010. Developing a pos-tagged corpus using existing tools. In *LREC 2010 Proceedings: Proceedings of the Workshop on "Creation and use of basic lexical resources for less-resourced languages"*.

Jahanbakhsh Nikoopour and Azin Kazemi. 2014. Vocabulary learning through digitized & non-digitized flashcards delivery. *Procedia - Social and Behavioral Sciences*, 98:1366–1373. Proceedings of the International Conference on Current Trends in ELT.

Eiríkur Rögnvaldsson. 2020. *A Short Overview of the Icelandic Sound System Pronunciation Variants and Phonetic Transcription.*

Eiríkur Rögnvaldsson, Hrafn Loftsson, Kristín Bjarnadóttir, Sigrún Helgadóttir, Anna Björk Nikulásdóttir, Matthew Whelpton, and Anton Karl Ingason. 2009. Icelandic language resources and technology: status and prospects. In *Proceedings of the NODALIDA 2009 Workshop Nordic Perspectives on the CLARIN Infrastructure of Language Resources. Odense, Denmark.*

Kara Sage, Michael Piazzini, IV John Charles Downey, and Sydney Ewing. 2020. Flip it or click it: Equivalent learning of vocabulary from paper, laptop, and smartphone flashcards. *Journal of Educational Technology Systems*, 49(2):145–169.

Norbert Schmitt. 2008. Review article: Instructed second language vocabulary learning. *Language Teaching Research*, 12(3):329–363.

Kerrick Staley. 2021. Genanki 0.10.1. `https://github.com/kerrickstaley/genanki.git`.

Norbert Stuhrmann. 2005. *The flacards class.* CTAN package version 0.1.1b.

Yihui Xie. 2021. *Knitr: A General-Purpose Package for Dynamic Report Generation in R.* R package version 1.31.

Leveraging Task Information in Grammatical Error Correction for Short Answer Assessment through Context-based Reranking

Ramon Ziai **Anna Karnysheva**

Department of Linguistics
University of Tübingen

{rziai,akrnshva}@sfs.uni-tuebingen.de

Abstract

One of the issues in automatically evaluating learner input in the context of Intelligent Tutoring Systems is learners' use of incorrect forms and non-standard language. Grammatical Error Correction (GEC) systems have emerged as a way of automatically correcting grammar and spelling mistakes, often by approaching the task as machine translation of individual sentences from non-standard to standard language. However, due to the inherent lack of context awareness, GEC systems often do not produce a contextually appropriate correction.

In this paper, we investigate how current neural GEC systems can be optimized for educationally relevant tasks such as Short Answer Assessment. We build on a recent GEC system and train a reranker based on context (e.g. similarity to prompt), task (e.g. type and format) and answer-level (e.g. language modeling) features on a Short Answer Assessment data set augmented with crowd worker corrections. Results show that our approach successfully gives preference to corrections that are closer to the reference.

1 Introduction

Grammatical Error Correction (GEC) is an active field of research, where the task is, given a potentially ungrammatical sentence, to compute a corrected version without changing the meaning Usually framed as a machine translation task with translation from the "ungrammatical" to the "grammatical" language. Statistical and (more recently) neural MT models are being used to output an n-best list of corrections for a given input sentence.

GEC overlaps with language learning in that there are educational applications of it, but a GEC system is by no means automatically an educational application. One of the reasons for this is that GEC systems try to correct a sentence in isolation, with no knowledge of the linguistic context or functional goal the sentence was uttered in. As a result, a GEC system often does not produce a contextually appropriate or likely correction, the way a language teacher or tutor would when interpreting a learner production in a task context. Consider the following example from an actual GEC system (S) on a student answer (A) to a question (Q) with a reference answer (R) in a Short Answer task:

Q: How much must Burbage pay for the play?
A: 1000 silver croins
S: 1000 silver croins
R: 1000 silver crowns

The system evidently does not resolve the creative but malformed word "croins" to either "crowns" or "coins", while for a human it would be immediately apparent that the student meant to say one of these.

In this paper, we present an attempt to contextualize Grammatical Error Correction for the task of Short Answer Assessment. We build on a recent GEC system by Kaneko et al. (2020) and make use of the fact that it outputs an n-best list of corrections which can be reranked. In order to obtain a data basis, we augment the Short Answer Assessment data set by Ziai et al. (2019) with reference grammar corrections from crowd workers using Amazon Mechanical Turk. We use this data basis to train a ranking approach combining context, task

Ramon Ziai and Anna Karnysheva 2021. Leveraging task information in grammatical error correction for short answer assessment through context-based reranking. *Proceedings of the 10th Workshop on Natural Language Processing for Computer Assisted Language Learning (NLP4CALL 2021)*. Linköping Electronic Conference Proceedings 177: 62–68.

and answer features in a gradient boosting model. Results show clear improvements for the reranked model in comparison with the original GEC system.

The paper is organized as follows: section 2 gives a brief overview of other work in reranking for GEC. In section 3 we present the data set and the crowd-based GEC extension to it, before describing the reranking approach in section 4. Section 5 then presents the GEC system we build on before we discuss the evaluation we performed in section 6. Finally, section 7 concludes the paper.

2 Related Work

Reranking hypotheses of GEC systems is not in itself a new idea and has followed in the wake of reranking for statistical machine translation (SMT). Mizumoto and Matsumoto (2016) implemented discriminative reranking for GEC based on an SMT system. They used syntactic and POS features in an averaged perceptron as the reranker, achieving a 2.1 increase in $F_{0.5}$ (40.0 vs. 37.9 on the CoNLL 2014 test data) over the original 1-best result of the SMT system.

Hoang et al. (2016) train an edit classifier on a combination of SMT (hypothesis rank), lexical, POS, local context and language model features to distinguish between valid and invalid edits based on an error-annotated learner corpus. This classifier is then used to score the edits of candidate hypotheses in n-best lists of an SMT-based GEC system and thus provides a reranking based on the total number of valid and invalid edits in each hypothesis. The authors report a modest improvement in $F_{0.5}$ (40.85 vs. 40.58 on the CoNLL test data) for 10-best reranking.

Yuan et al. (2016) describe an approach where they combine SMT (decoder score & hypothesis rank) and different language model features in a ranking SVM to rerank the output of an SMT-based GEC system. In contrast to the other approaches, the authors pay special attention to evaluation metrics and optimize their ranking approach on I-measure (Felice and Briscoe, 2015), a metric that includes all confusion matrix counts instead of $F_{0.5}$. They report an improvement of .75 in $F_{0.5}$ (38.08 vs. 37.33 on the CoNLL-2014 test data) when reranking the 10 top hypotheses of their GEC system.

In a more recent approach, Chollampatt and Ng (2018) perform rescoring of the final correction candidates using edit operation (insertion, deletion, substitution) and language model features as part of their neural GEC system based on a convolutional encoder-decoder network. They report an $F_{0.5}$ improvement of 4.8 (54.13 vs 49.33) on the CoNLL-2014 test data, with the language model features being particularly effective.

In a different but related research direction, with the introduction of neural approaches there have also been attempts to incorporate context directly into GEC systems. Chollampatt et al. (2019) present a model capable of incorporating cross-sentence information with the help of an auxiliary encoder that encodes previous sentences. They report statistically significant increases in $F_{0.5}$ on the CoNLL-2014 test data when comparing with the non-contextual baseline.

All of these approaches have in common that they try to solve the problem of GEC in a general way, without taking into account what functional goal the language to be corrected is produced for. In contrast, our attempt in this paper is to incorporate the downstream task of Short Answer Assessment directly into GEC by reranking GEC hypotheses based on features specific to the Short Answer setting.

3 Data

Standard GEC data sets tend to be short essays or other free writing tasks, where explicit task context is not readily available. To be able to evaluate GEC approaches in Short Answer Assessment, we need a data set from the latter task with the ground truth (grammatical reference corrections) of the former.

3.1 Short Answer Assessment Data Set

We use the data set introduced by Ziai et al. (2019). It consists of 3,829 answers to 123 questions in 25 tasks, where each task is either a reading or a listening comprehension task. The answers were produced by German students of English in the 7th grade as part of their normal school curriculum. On average, they wrote 7.11 tokens per answer. The answers were annotated by a teacher with respect to whether they are acceptable in terms of content (62.05%) or not (37.95%). Ziai et al. (2019) show that spelling correction is effective in this data set as a preprocessing step for Short Answer Assessment, indicating that form errors are in fact quite common here. This makes it a good test bed for our purposes in this paper.

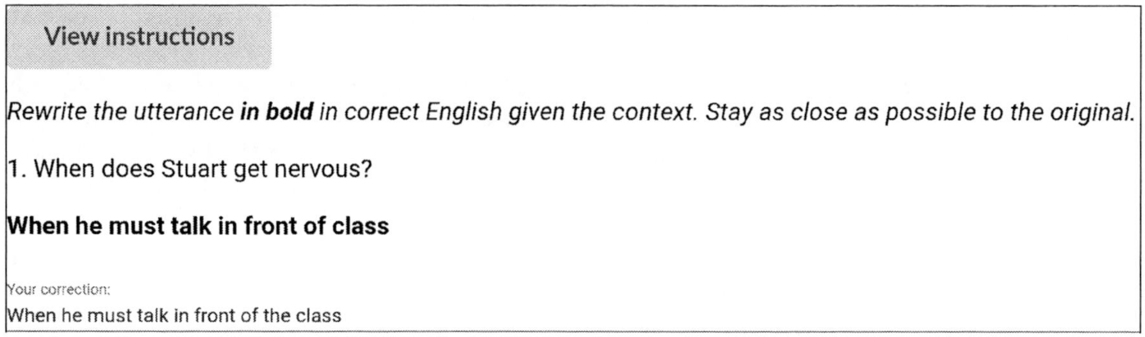

Figure 1: Example crowd task in Amazon Mechanical Turk

3.2 Crowd-sourced gold standard for GEC

Since no reference corrections for the data set were available and a full error annotation by experts was both unnecessary and beyond the scope of this paper, we decided to use Amazon Mechanical Turk to obtain reference corrections from linguistically untrained crowd workers. There has not been extensive work on crowd-sourcing for GEC so far, a fact that Pavlick et al. (2014) attribute to the difficulty of performing automatic quality control for diverging candidate corrections of workers. While general-purpose GEC may not be constrained enough for crowd-sourcing to be successful, Boyd (2018) showed that restriction in terms of context and task improves inter-annotator agreement in word-level normalization for expert annotators. We therefore assume that this insight can be applied to crowd-sourcing GEC as well.

We used the setup shown in Figure 1, where workers were shown the prompt in addition to the student answer, and then needed to come up with a free-text correction, with the original student answer as default. For each of the 3,829 answers, we obtained five crowd corrections. Workers needed 32 seconds on average and were paid 0.03$ per answer. We only used workers who have shown reliability and consistence in other Mechanical Turk tasks (so-called 'Master Workers').[2]

To obtain a reference from the five corrections for each answer, we made use of the corrections' string similarity to each other: we determined the correction with the largest average token overlap to the other crowd corrections. The idea behind this approach is to avoid picking idiosyncratic or erroneous outlier corrections and instead choose one that most other crowd workers agree with. We leave other more involved strategies to future research, as well as a detailed annotator agreement analysis, which is non-trivial in GEC (cf. Pavlick et al. 2014) and thus outside the scope of this paper.

To support such further research at the interface of GEC and Short Answer Grading, we make the compiled corpus available upon request under a CC-BY-NC-SA license.

4 Reranking

In this section, we describe the reranking approach we use in this paper. Reranking has traditionally been done extensively in the area of (web) search engines, in order to optimize or personalize a given list of results (see e.g. Page et al. 1998). Where in web search the task is to reorder a list of search results for a given query, in our problem we are dealing with a list of candidate corrections for a given natural language utterance.

4.1 Learning Algorithm

For the learning algorithm with which to combine features of candidate corrections and learn a task-specific preference function, we chose LightGBM (Ke et al., 2017), a framework which includes ranking versions of various tree-based learning algorithms (gradient boosting, random forests etc.) besides the usual classification and regression approaches.

In addition to feature vectors for each correction candidate, LightGBM takes as input grouping information expressing which corrections to treat as a set to be ranked. We obtain the 10 best corrections from a neural GEC system (see section 5) as input for the algorithm to rerank.

The final ingredient for the reranker is a numerical dependent variable expressing the quality of each correction. We use the crowd

[2] https://www.mturk.com/worker/help#what_is_master_worker

reference discussed in the previous section to calculate Weighted Accuracy based on a token-level alignment (calculated using ERRANT, Felice et al. 2016) of source answer, candidate correction and reference correction following Yuan et al. (2016). Weighted Accuracy (*WAcc*) is defined as follows[3]:

$$WAcc = \frac{w \cdot TP + TN}{w \cdot (TP + FP) + TN + FN - (w+1) \cdot \frac{FPN}{2}}$$

Through the use of the weight w (we use $w = 2$), *WAcc* "rewards correction more than preservation" and "penalises unnecessary corrections more than uncorrected errors" (Felice and Briscoe, 2015). In contrast to $F_{0.5}$, it also takes into account true negatives (TN) which in GEC correspond to successfully preserved correct input forms, and thus also yields a non-zero score for corrections that do not alter the source sentence.

4.2 Features

The overall idea of our feature set is to combine answer-level features (e.g. language modeling) with contextual features (e.g. similarity to prompt) in an attempt to balance global language features with task-specific ones. We describe the features in detail below.

Original GEC system rank We include the information on how the GEC system (see section 5) ranked a particular correction candidate from 1 to 10.

Task characteristics The Short Answer data set (see section 3) contains information on task type (reading vs. listening comprehension), task format (question-answer vs. fill-in-the-blanks) and expected input type (word, phrase or sentence). We encode these categorical variables as one-hot features.

String similarity We use the textdistance package[4] to calculate nine different string similarity measures covering edit-based, sequence-based, phonetic and token-based distance of candidate corrections to prompt, original answer and target answer, resulting in a total of 27 features. The rationale is to make the reranker prefer candidate corrections that are closer to the task context.

BERT-based similarity To account for semantic similarity, we use BERT-base (Devlin et al., 2019) through bert-as-service (Xiao, 2018) to obtain sentence embeddings and calculate cosine similarity again between candidate corrections and prompt, original answer and target answer (three features).

Language Modeling Similar to previous approaches, we include a language modeling feature. We do so by obtaining the smoothed log probability for each token in a candidate correction using spaCy[5] and summing over the log probabilities to get a probability for the correction sequence.

TF-IDF Since corrections with terms that are important in the reading/listening text should be more relevant than corrections without such terms, we calculate TF-IDF for all words in all reading/listening texts and encode this term weighting information in one feature as the average of TF-IDF values of words in a given candidate correction.

5 GEC System

Reranking presupposes a GEC system capable of producing multiple hypotheses for a given input sentence. Beyond this requirement, the only other desirable characteristics are competitive performance and ease of use. Any GEC system that satisfies these requirements can in principle be used.

For our experiments in this paper, we chose to use bert-gec (Kaneko et al., 2020) because it is sufficiently documented and currently one of the top five GEC systems with available source code. It uses the transformer architecture proposed by Vaswani et al. (2017) and extends it by fine-tuning an additional BERT model on a GEC corpus and using its output as additional features in the GEC transformer model.

Following the procedure in the published bert-gec code[6], we trained the system on the WI-LOCNESS train data set (Bryant et al., 2019). For reference, we also evaluated the obtained model on the corresponding validation set,[7] achieving an $F_{0.5}$ of 55.6 as computed by ERRANT. Grundkiewicz et al. (2019) report an $F_{0.5}$ of 53.0 on this set using their slightly older approach, which won the BEA 2019 shared task on GEC. The so trained bert-gec model was used to get a 10-best list of corrections

[3] *FPN* denotes cases where a word was altered differently in the candidate and the reference translation.

[4] `https://github.com/life4/textdistance`

[5] `https://spacy.io/`

[6] `https://github.com/kanekomasahiro/bert-gec`

[7] The test set remains hidden by the BEA-19 shared task organizers to enable further task submissions.

for each of the 3,829 short answers, resulting in 38,290 corrections to be ranked.

In contrast to the Short Answer data we use in this paper, the utterances in WI-LOCNESS come from a different age group (college students) and also partly from native speakers of English. It is therefore fair to assume that the use of the model for our purpose in this paper represents an out-of-domain scenario. Indeed, as we will see in section 6, performance drops significantly for bert-gec on the data set used in this paper.

6 Evaluation

We now turn to describing the evaluation of the reranking approach on the Short Answer data introduced in section 3. After outlining the evaluation setup, we proceed to reporting and discussing the results we obtained.

6.1 Setup

For a fair evaluation setup, we split the Short Answer data into train (50%), validation (20%) and test (30%), making sure that all corrections of a particular 10-best list end up in the same portion of the data set. The validation set was used for hyperparameter optimization and the test set for the evaluation of the reranker trained on the training set.

We compared three systems: a baseline with the uncorrected answer, the original best correction as determined by bert-gec, and the best correction as determined by the reranker. In addition to the widely used $F_{0.5}$, we also report *WAcc* since $F_{0.5}$ is not always meaningful.

6.2 Results

Table 1 presents the overall results. Our first observation is that the baseline of uncorrected text is quite low in this data set, meaning that necessary corrections are quite frequent according to the crowd reference. Looking at the performance of bert-gec, it is striking to see that it drops by roughly 20 points compared to the same model's result on in-domain test data ($F_{0.5} = 55.6$). It seems clear that although the advent of neural models has considerably improved performance in GEC, this improvement is not necessarily generalizable to other domains.

System	*WAcc*	$F_{0.5}$
Uncorrected	29.11	0.0
bert-gec	75.98	35.42
Reranked	**80.80**	**37.42**

Table 1: Overall evaluation results

On the positive side, we observe a clear improvement of the reranker in both *WAcc* and $F_{0.5}$ when compared to the original bert-gec. This shows that our reranking approach specific to Short Answer Assessment is successful in preferring corrections that fit the context.

We also performed a more detailed analysis of error types annotated automatically using ERRANT. Table 2 shows the ten most frequent error types[8] in the data, along with the $F_{0.5}$ of bert-gec and the reranked model, respectively.

Error type	#	%	bert-gec	Reranked
PUNCT	316	26.03	**39.72**	26.75
ORTH	191	15.73	23.32	**31.28**
SPELL	189	15.57	76.67	**78.18**
OTHER	140	11.53	18.67	**19.23**
VERB	49	4.04	44.97	**50.34**
MORPH	44	3.62	23.15	**23.44**
DET	43	3.54	17.02	**19.08**
PREP	39	3.21	26.07	**28.46**
VERB:TENSE	37	3.05	40.08	**47.45**
VERB:SVA	36	2.97	**75.00**	70.95
...			...	
Total	1214	100	35.42	**37.42**

Table 2: $F_{0.5}$ for 10 most frequent error types, with each type's absolute (#) and relative frequency (%)

Apart from a negative result in punctuation errors, likely caused by crowd workers being unsure whether to apply punctuation in their corrections or not, we see improvements in most other frequent error types. Among others, verb-related and orthographic errors in particular seem to benefit from the reranking. Both are relevant areas for language learners, so it is encouraging to see that such areas can be improved by our approach.

More generally, it is somewhat striking to see that the majority of errors observed is classified by ERRANT as relatively surface-oriented (punctuation, spelling, orthography, etc). While a full GEC approach may seem somewhat oversized for these kinds of errors, correcting them is often context-dependent and thus outside the reach of a standard spell checking approach.

Taking a closer look at our features for reranking, we performed feature ablation tests for each of

[8]See Bryant et al. (2017, p. 795) for a description of the error types annotated by ERRANT.

the groups discussed in section 4. The results are shown in Table 3.

Feature set	*WAcc*	$F_{0.5}$
Full	80.80	37.42
- original GEC rank	80.97	36.27
- task characteristics	80.92	38.02
- string similarity	77.65	35.54
- BERT-based similarity	**80.98**	**38.37**
- language modeling	80.74	37.29
- TF-IDF	80.69	37.51

Table 3: Feature ablation tests

Interestingly, the full feature set is not the best performing model. Instead, removing BERT-based cosine similarity features improves both *WAcc* and $F_{0.5}$. This seems to suggest that the deeper semantic similarity offered by BERT sentence embeddings is actually counter-productive to the more surface-oriented goal of picking the optimal correction from the 10-best set.

This suspicion is further strengthened when observing that removing the string similarity features results in the largest drop in performance across all feature groups. These more surface-oriented features, expressing how close a correction string is to the prompt, target, and student answer strings, successfully encode Short Answer task characteristics, approximating the expectation a teacher would form when interpreting a student answer in the context of a Short Answer task.

7 Conclusion

We presented the first GEC reranking approach based on context and task, designed to tune correction for the purpose of Short Answer Assessment. To do so, we augmented an existing Short Answer data set with reference corrections using crowd workers. Results of our reranking approach trained on a combination of context, task and answer features show that it is effective in preferring contextually more appropriate grammar and spelling corrections.

Applying an existing competitive GEC system "out of the box", it also becomes clear that GEC systems need to develop better generalizability: we observed a 20-point drop in $F_{0.5}$ when applying a model trained on a standard GEC corpus to Short Answer Assessment data. This may be due to different learner/speaker populations, or different nature and frequency of errors picked up by the GEC system.

We also observed that performance is not uniform across error types. For real-life educational applications, a focus on specific error types known to be corrected with high reliability could thus be a way towards using current GEC systems in practice.

In future work, we plan to investigate whether the improvement observed in our reranking approach carries over to Short Answer Grading in an extrinsic evaluation setting, where answers to be scored are first corrected by the reranked GEC model.

In a slightly different strand, the reranked model could also be used as the basis of a feedback tool, providing context-based suggestions for student utterances in foreign language exercises, and possibly also information on the nature of the grammar and spelling mistakes observed.

Acknowledgments

We are very grateful for the helpful comments of two anonymous reviewers. This work was done as part of the ISAAC project (`https://www.uni-tuebingen.de/isaac`), funded as part of the Excellence Strategy of the German Federal and State Governments.

References

Adriane Boyd. 2018. Normalization in context: Inter-annotator agreement for meaning-based target hypothesis annotation. In *Proceedings of the 7th workshop on NLP for Computer Assisted Language Learning*, pages 10–22, Stockholm, Sweden. LiU Electronic Press.

Christopher Bryant, Mariano Felice, Øistein E. Andersen, and Ted Briscoe. 2019. The BEA-2019 shared task on grammatical error correction. In *Proceedings of the Fourteenth Workshop on Innovative Use of NLP for Building Educational Applications*, pages 52–75, Florence, Italy. Association for Computational Linguistics.

Christopher Bryant, Mariano Felice, and Ted Briscoe. 2017. Automatic annotation and evaluation of error types for grammatical error correction. In *Proceedings of the 55th Annual Meeting of the Association for Computational Linguistics (Volume 1: Long Papers)*, pages 793–805, Vancouver, Canada. Association for Computational Linguistics.

Shamil Chollampatt and Hwee Tou Ng. 2018. A multilayer convolutional encoder-decoder neural network for grammatical error correction. In *Thirty-Second*

AAAI Conference on Artificial Intelligence, pages 5755–5762.

Shamil Chollampatt, Weiqi Wang, and Hwee Tou Ng. 2019. Cross-sentence grammatical error correction. In *Proceedings of the 57th Annual Meeting of the Association for Computational Linguistics*, pages 435–445, Florence, Italy. Association for Computational Linguistics.

Jacob Devlin, Ming-Wei Chang, Kenton Lee, and Kristina Toutanova. 2019. BERT: Pre-training of deep bidirectional transformers for language understanding.

Mariano Felice and Ted Briscoe. 2015. Towards a standard evaluation method for grammatical error detection and correction. In *Proceedings of the 2015 Conference of the North American Chapter of the Association for Computational Linguistics: Human Language Technologies*, pages 578–587, Denver, Colorado. Association for Computational Linguistics.

Mariano Felice, Christopher Bryant, and Ted Briscoe. 2016. Automatic extraction of learner errors in ESL sentences using linguistically enhanced alignments. In *Proceedings of COLING 2016, the 26th International Conference on Computational Linguistics: Technical Papers*, pages 825–835, Osaka, Japan. The COLING 2016 Organizing Committee.

Roman Grundkiewicz, Marcin Junczys-Dowmunt, and Kenneth Heafield. 2019. Neural grammatical error correction systems with unsupervised pre-training on synthetic data. In *Proceedings of the Fourteenth Workshop on Innovative Use of NLP for Building Educational Applications*, pages 252–263, Florence, Italy. Association for Computational Linguistics.

Duc Tam Hoang, Shamil Chollampatt, and Hwee Tou Ng. 2016. Exploiting n-best hypotheses to improve an smt approach to grammatical error correction. In *Proceedings of the Twenty-Fifth International Joint Conference on Artificial Intelligence*, IJCAI'16, page 2803–2809. AAAI Press.

Masahiro Kaneko, Masato Mita, Shun Kiyono, Jun Suzuki, and Kentaro Inui. 2020. Encoder-decoder models can benefit from pre-trained masked language models in grammatical error correction. In *Proceedings of the 58th Annual Meeting of the Association for Computational Linguistics*, pages 4248–4254, Online. Association for Computational Linguistics.

Guolin Ke, Qi Meng, Thomas Finley, Taifeng Wang, Wei Chen, Weidong Ma, Qiwei Ye, and Tie-Yan Liu. 2017. LightGBM: A highly efficient gradient boosting decision tree. In *Advances in Neural Information Processing Systems*, volume 30, pages 3146–3154. Curran Associates, Inc.

Tomoya Mizumoto and Yuji Matsumoto. 2016. Discriminative reranking for grammatical error correction with statistical machine translation. In *Proceedings of the 2016 Conference of the North American Chapter of the Association for Computational Linguistics: Human Language Technologies*, pages 1133–1138, San Diego, California. Association for Computational Linguistics.

Lawrence Page, Sergey Brin, Rajeev Motwani, and Terry Winograd. 1998. The pagerank citation ranking: Bringing order to the web. Technical report, Stanford Digital Libraries.

Ellie Pavlick, Rui Yan, and Chris Callison-Burch. 2014. Crowdsourcing for grammatical error correction. In *Proceedings of the Companion Publication of the 17th ACM Conference on Computer Supported Cooperative Work & Social Computing*, CSCW Companion '14, page 209–212, New York, NY, USA. Association for Computing Machinery.

Ashish Vaswani, Noam Shazeer, Niki Parmar, Jakob Uszkoreit, Llion Jones, Aidan N. Gomez, Lukasz Kaiser, and Illia Polosukhin. 2017. Attention is all you need.

Han Xiao. 2018. bert-as-service. `https://github.com/hanxiao/bert-as-service`.

Zheng Yuan, Ted Briscoe, and Mariano Felice. 2016. Candidate re-ranking for SMT-based grammatical error correction. In *Proceedings of the 11th Workshop on Innovative Use of NLP for Building Educational Applications*, pages 256–266, San Diego, CA. Association for Computational Linguistics.

Ramon Ziai, Florian Nuxoll, Kordula De Kuthy, Björn Rudzewitz, and Detmar Meurers. 2019. The impact of spelling correction and task context on short answer assessment for intelligent tutoring systems. In *Proceedings of the 8th Workshop on NLP for Computer Assisted Language Learning*, pages 93–99, Turku, Finland. ACL.

Association for Computational Linguistics
209 N. Eighth Street
Stroudsburg, Pennsylvania 18360

CURRAN ASSOCIATES INC.
proceedings.com

ISBN 978-1-7138-9189-5

9 781713 891895

15th Workshop on Building and Using Comparable Corpora (BUCC 2022)

Held at LREC 2022

Marseille, France
25 June 2022